Terrific 2x4 Furniture

Terrific 2x4 Furniture

Building Stylish Furniture from Standard Lumber

Stevie Henderson *with* **Mark Baldwin**

Sterling Publishing Co., Inc. New York
A Sterling/Lark Book

DEDICATION

To Jessica and Mike Bates
In their first year of forever

EDITOR
Thomas Stender

ART DIRECTOR
Chris Bryant

PHOTOGRAPHY
Evan Bracken

ILLUSTRATIONS
Thomas Stender

PRODUCTION ASSISTANT
and ILLUSTRATIONS
Hannes Charen

10 9 8 7 6 5 4 3 2

Published in 2002 by Lark Books, a division of
Sterling Publishing Company, Inc.
387 Park Avenue South, New York, NY 10016
©1998 by Stevie Henderson
Distributed in Canada by Sterling Publishing
c/o Canadian Manda Group, One Atlantic Avenue, Suite 105
Toronto, Ontario, Canada M6K 3E7
Distributed in Great Britain by Chrysalis Books
64 Brewery Road, London N7 9NT, England
Distributed in Australia by Capricorn Link (Australia) Pty. Ltd.
P.O. Box 704, Windsor, NSW 2756, Australia

Printed in Hong Kong
All rights reserved

Sterling ISBN 0-8069-7349-8

CONTENTS

INTRODUCTION

IF YOU'VE EVER THOUGHT TO YOURSELF, "I would love to be able to build that!" then you already possess the most important woodworking ability—desire. Woodworking is not a mysterious process, and it doesn't take special ability or special intelligence. What it takes is the desire to learn, attention to detail, and a little preliminary knowledge—which is why we wrote this book.

The projects in this book are designed to be built by beginners. There are no reproduction antiques in these pages, and a minimum of tools is required. These designs circumvent the need for advanced woodworking skills. They also take advantage of premade products available at building supply stores. Still not convinced? Turn to one of the shorter projects and read through the instructions. We think you'll see for yourself that you can make it. So dig right in! You'll then be on your way to building larger and more complex projects—and, inevitably, you'll begin designing your own!

We've built coordinated projects for each room of the house and photographed them together to give you a sense of how they complement each other. Select and complete one project or furnish your entire home! Build just the dining table, or add a buffet to the room. We've also included some "occasional" projects, go-anywhere furniture that can be added to almost any area in your home.

We hope you enjoy making and living with these pieces as much as we have!

TOOLS, TECHNIQUES, AND MATERIALS

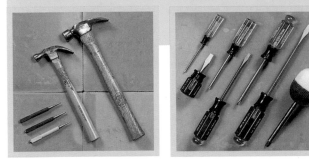

TOOLS

IF YOU WANT TO SAVE MONEY and build sturdy, good-looking, and practical furniture pieces for your home, but you have no experience working with wood—this book is for you. The instructions are written for someone who owns a limited number of tools and has little or no woodworking experience. Woodworking is not difficult. If you can drive a nail and cut a piece of wood to length, you can produce the projects in this book. Woodworking, like any other endeavor, requires some patience and a little introductory knowledge to get started. We suggest that you read through "Tools, Techniques, and Materials" before beginning any project.

If you are an accomplished woodworker who works in a fully equipped shop of stationary power tools, please bear in mind that these instructions are geared to the beginner. Not all of them may translate easily and safely to your particular power tools. You may be accustomed to somewhat different methods from those specified here. We suggest, therefore, that you alter the instructions to accommodate your more advanced tools and knowledge. Know the capabilities of your tools and don't exceed them.

No matter what your experience level is, we know that you can make these projects. When you have completed one of the simpler pieces, you will want to make another which may require a technique you haven't tried. You will build your skills while making special pieces of furniture for your home. The best part comes after that last coat of varnish has dried and you place the finished project in your house. When someone admires your handiwork (and they will), you can simply say, "Thank you. I made it myself."

If you are just beginning in woodworking, you may have the idea that it costs thousands of dollars to be involved in woodworking. Not true! Unless they are independently wealthy, most woodworkers start using hand tools and gradually add to their shop over time. Obviously, there weren't too many power tools when Louis XV's furniture craftsmen were at work—all of history's magnificent furniture was built using only hand tools. The obvious reason for power tools is that they get the job done faster.

Our goal is to create a good-looking piece of furniture in the least amount of time. So over the years we have added power tools that cut the time required to complete the job and require a lot less physical effort. We use a power drill rather than a screwdriver and a circular saw rather than a hand saw. A good approach is to add a tool to your workshop each time you build a large project. You will still save a substantial amount of money compared to purchasing the item in a store, and you will have the tool for the next project.

The projects in this book require some basic tools that, if you don't already own them, make useful additions to any household. Some tools, such as a saw and a set of screwdrivers, are needed for every project, but others, such as a staple gun, are required for only a few pieces (and even then you may be able to find a "work-around"). You may want to choose your first project according to the tools you have available. To determine which tools you will need, read through the instructions before starting a project. The tools required for the projects in this book make a good starting set of woodworking equipment.

If you are starting from scratch, buy the best tools you can afford. A bargain screwdriver that falls apart after inserting three screws is not much of a bargain, and the resulting frustration is not worth the two-dollar savings. Look for the manufacturer's warranty when purchasing tools. If they offer a lifetime guarantee, it's a safe bet that it's a good tool.

Tool Kit

BASIC TOOLS

- Working surface that is smooth and level

- Measuring tools: tape measure, level, combination square

- Hammers: claw hammer, tack hammer, nail set

- Screwdrivers: assortment of flathead and Phillips sizes

- Saws: combination saw, or rip saw and crosscut saw, coping saw

- Drill: hand or power drill and a variety of bits

- Clamps: two "quick clamps," two wood hand clamps, some 2-inch spring clamps

- Sanding tools: sanding block and assortment of sandpaper from fine to coarse

- Safety equipment: goggles, dust mask, hearing protection (use with all power tools)

OPTIONAL TOOLS

- Woodworking vise or portable vise/work table

- Measuring tools: framing square

- Clamps: two "C" clamps, web clamp, two light-duty bar clamps, two pipe clamps

- Saws: saber saw, circular saw and a selection of blades

- Chisels: ¼-inch, ¾-inch, and 1-inch wide

- Planes: low-angle block plane, bench plane

- Finishing sander

- Router

- Power miter box

ADVANCED TOOLS

- Belt sander

- Table saw

- Band saw

- Drill press

See the chart, "Tool Kit," at left, which lists our recommendations for a basic set of tools and for more advanced equipment.

As with most hobbies, when you purchase your equipment you should consider your physical size and ability. A golf club or a tennis racquet must be matched to the person using it. In the same way, a physically large person may be able to use a very large hammer. While it is true that the larger hammer will drive the nail into the wood faster, it doesn't mean very much if you are able to swing a heavier hammer only twice before you feel your arm going weak from the strain. So try before you buy! Lift the tool a number of times before you decide that it is for you. The same philosophy applies to power tools. It requires a great deal of strength to control a 4-inch-wide belt sander, but almost anyone can use a 2-inch-wide sander.

A hammer and saw probably come to mind when someone discusses woodworking. However, other tools are just as important. A solid work surface, a ready supply of clamps, and the right sanding equipment can make woodworking an enjoyable pursuit—the lack of them can spell complete frustration.

Work Surface

Although most people would not put it at the top of the list, one of the most important tools in woodworking is a work surface that is smooth and level. If you construct a project on an uneven work surface, chances are that your table legs will be uneven or the cabinet top will slope downhill. Your work surface doesn't have to be a professional-quality mahogany workbench—it just has to be level and even. It can be as simple as an old door (flush, not paneled) or a piece of thick plywood supported by sawhorses.

To level your work surface, simply set a fairly long level in various places on the surface and turn it so that it faces in several directions. Also stand back and sight along the surface to make sure it isn't twisted. Then shim the surfaces with thicknesses of wood to lift the surface enough to be perfectly level. Be sure to attach the shim with glue and nails or screws to make certain that it stays in place while you work.

Clockwise from top-right: spring clamps, light-duty bar clamps, wood clamp, pipe clamps, C-clamps

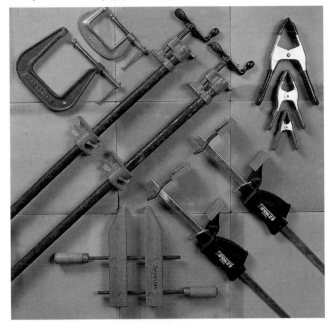

Clamps

Clamps are an absolute must for woodworking. They are used to apply pressure and hold joints together until the glue sets, and they are valuable aids when assembling a project. A single person can assemble a large project by using clamps—a job that might otherwise require the concerted effort of two or more people. When you buy clamps, it is advisable to get two clamps of the same type, because you almost always use them in pairs to provide even pressure on the work.

When you apply clamps, always insert a scrap piece of wood between the clamp and your work to act as a cushion. That way you will avoid leaving clamp marks on the surface of your project.

There have been some fairly recent improvements in woodworking clamps. A new type looks like a regular bar clamp, but instead of tightening it by turning a screw mechanism, you squeeze its double handle as you would with a caulk gun. This makes these clamps especially useful since they can be operated with one hand. They also have a quick-release mechanism. I recommend them for a beginner, since they are easy to use, work well, and come in a variety of lengths.

Spring clamps come in very handy for quickly holding a piece of wood while you saw or for keeping two thin boards positioned. The 2-inch size is most useful because you can operate it with one hand.

Old-fashioned wood clamps are a nice addition to your workshop. They are extremely versatile since they can be adjusted to clamp offsetting surfaces.

"C" clamps are inexpensive and useful for many woodworking applications. One end of their C-shaped frame is fixed; the other end is fitted with a threaded rod and swivel pad that can be clamped tightly across an opening ranging from zero to several inches or more, depending upon the size of the clamp. They can hold two thicknesses of wood together, secure a piece of wood to a work surface, and perform many other functions.

Bar clamps and pipe clamps can be used to hold assemblies together temporarily while you add the fasteners, as well as to apply pressure to laminates. While the two types look very much alike and function the same way, pipe clamps are significantly less expensive. You buy the fittings separately, and they can be used with various lengths of pipe, depending upon the need. You can also buy rubber "shoes" that fit over the pipe-clamp fittings, which will eliminate clamp marks on the wood. Remember to put pieces of plastic or waxed paper between the pipes and any glue lines they cross, because a chemical reaction between the glue and the pipe can leave a dark stain on your wood.

Web clamps (or band clamps) are used for clamping such things as chairs or drawers, where a uniform pressure needs to be exerted completely around a project. They consist of a continuous band with an attached metal mechanism that can be ratcheted to pull the band tightly around the object.

Measuring

If you have been involved with woodworking at all, you have probably heard the expression, "measure twice, cut once." And it is always worth repeating. If you measure accurately and cut carefully to that measurement, your project will fit together perfectly during final assembly. And accurate cutting depends on accurate measurements, so a quality measuring tool is a sound investment. A wide steel tape rule is a good choice for most projects. A narrow tape will bend more easily along the length of a board and will be less accurate. A quality tape measure has its "hook" mounted so it can slide exactly the thickness of

MEASURING TOOLS. Clockwise from top: carpenter's square, combination square, adjustable bevel, electronic level, and conventional level

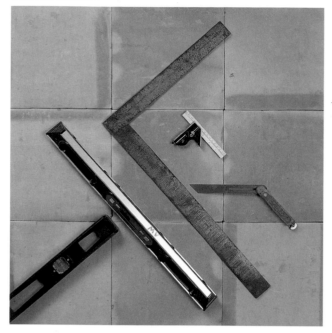

TECHNIQUES

Cutting

Keep in mind that every saw blade has a thickness (called a kerf) which is removed from the wood when you cut (whence cometh the gigantic amount of sawdust that accumulates when you make a project). When you measure and mark a board, measure precisely and use a sharp pencil. When you cut the board at your mark, set the saw so that the blade will exactly remove the waste side of the mark. You should try to remove just one-half of your pencil line.

A piece of wood may be either ripped (cut along the length of the board) or crosscut (cut across the width of the board). There are specific hand tools for each procedure. A rip saw has teeth designed for cutting along the length of board, with the grain. It comes with 4½ through 7 points per inch, the latter being the smoothest cut. The crosscut saw is made to cut across the grain. Crosscut saws are available with 7 through 12 points per inch, depending on how coarse or fine you wish the cut to be. The greater the number, the smoother (and the slower) the cut.

the hook. Therefore, it can be just as accurate for inside and outside measurements. Consistently use the same measuring device throughout the cutting process. Unless you have precise measuring tools, any two instruments may vary enough to give you slightly different measurements.

If you are cutting a length of wood to fit between two existing pieces in an assembly, there is an even more accurate method. After you square off the wood you are cutting, simply hold it up to the actual space, and mark it for cutting.

A straightedge is a handy woodworking tool for quick measurements. An ordinary steel ruler, 12 to 24 inches long, is sufficient.

An adjustable bevel is valuable for establishing bevel angles. The steel blade pivots and slides within a handle, and can be locked in position to form an angle. It is used to check and transfer bevels and mitered ends.

Squares are versatile and essential tools in woodworking. The most commonly used types are the framing square (or carpenter's square) and the combination square. In addition to their obvious use for marking a cutting line on a board and obtaining a right angle, squares can be used to check the outer or inner squareness of a joint, to guide a saw through a cut, and much more.

CUTTING TOOLS. Clockwise from top-right: circular saw, circular saw squaring jig, coping saw and blades, carpenter's handsaw, backsaw, miter box and saw, and electric jig saw

Probably the most popular power cutting tool is the circular saw. The blade can be adjusted to cut at a 90-degree or 45-degree angle or any angle in between. While saw blades for power tools are also designed for ripping and crosscutting, the most practical blade for general woodworking is a combination blade. It rips and crosscuts with equal ease. However, when you want especially smooth results, a specialized blade can be worthwhile. Carbide tipped blades are more expensive, but well worth the cost since they last much longer than regular blades.

The hand-held jig or saber saw is used to cut curves, shapes, and large holes in panels or boards up to 1½ inch in thickness. Its cutting action comes from a narrow reciprocating "bayonet" blade that moves up and down very quickly. The best saber saws have a variable speed control and an orbital blade action which swings the cutting edge forward into the work and back again during the blade's up-and-down cycle. A dust blower keeps the sawdust away from the cut.

A power miter saw is a favorite tool of mine. It can be used to efficiently cut boards to length and can be adjusted both horizontally and vertically from 0 to 45 degrees. It is especially useful for cutting 45-degree miters.

When you are cutting either lumber or plywood, note the type of cut that your tool is making, and use it to your advantage. For example, circular saws and saber saws cut on the upstroke, so they may leave ragged edges on the upper surface of your wood. When using these saws, you should position the wood with the better surface facing down.

Certain types of cuts, such as hollowing out a section of wood, are done with chisels. Using a chisel well takes some practice, but it is worth the effort because chisels can perform unique woodworking tasks. Always work with sharp chisels. For your first purchase, choose at least two sizes— one narrow and one about an inch wide.

CHISELS

PLANES. Left: surform tool. Right: low-angle block plane.

If you need to "shave" just a little off the end or along the edge of a board, a plane is the appropriate tool. Again, buy a quality plane, and practice with it until you become fairly proficient. We use a low-angle block plane with a blade that is kept very sharp. You can use it with one hand and the fact that the blade is set at a low angle means that it will plane even end grain.

Wood Joints

There are hundreds of different kinds of wood joints. They range in complexity from the plainest butt joint to incredibly intricate and time-consuming ones. The projects in this book are constructed with only the simplest joints, secured with glue and either nails or screws.

EDGE-TO-EDGE JOINT

This joint is used when laminating boards together edge to edge to obtain a wider piece of wood. To ensure a perfect meeting between boards, a minuscule amount should be ripped from the first edge of each board. Then flip the board widthwise to rip the second edge in order to ensure complementary angles and a flat glued surface. Apply glue to the adjoining edges and clamp the boards together.

Apply even clamping pressure along the length of the piece. The boards should be firmly clamped, but not so tightly that all of the glue is forced out or that the lamination starts to bow across its width. On a long lamination, extra boards may be placed above and below the lamination, across the width, and those boards clamped with "C" clamps or wood clamps. It is a good idea to put a piece of plastic or waxed paper between the workpiece and any wood clamped across the joints. This will eliminate the clamped board becoming a permanent part of the finished lamination. Wipe off any excess glue that is squeezed out in the clamping process.

Edge-To-Edge Joint

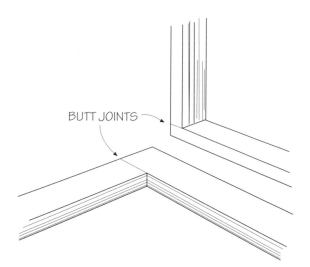

BUT JOINTS

BUTT JOINT

This is the simplest of joints, where one board abuts another at a right angle. This method offers the least holding power of any joint. It must be reinforced with some kind of fastener, usually screws.

MITER

A miter is a angle cut across the width of a board. It is used to join the ends of two pieces of wood at an angle without exposing the end grain of either piece. A mitered joint must also be reinforced with nails or screws. The angle most often cut is 45 degrees, which is used to construct a right angle when two mitered boards are joined together. The difference between a perfect miter and a none-too-perfect miter is the care in the measurement.

When cutting and applying molding, begin at one end, cut the first piece and attach it. Then cut the first angle on the second piece, hold it in place, and mark the cut (and the direction of that cut) on the other end. Since you are usually switching directions of 45-degree angles on each successive cut, this method avoids confusion. Attach the second piece, and continue the process for each subsequent piece. A helpful tip to make your miter joints look more perfect than they are is to firmly rub the length of the completed joint with the side of a pencil to smooth the two edges together.

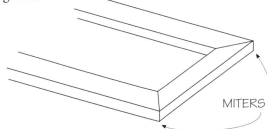

MITERS

Miters on Crown Moldings

Crown moldings, those which have curves on one face and two bevels on the other, can be tricky to miter. We have come up with a simple, shop-made jig to make this process much easier. To make the fabulous Crown Molding Mitering Jig, follow these steps:

1. Cut two bases from 1 x 6 pine, each measuring 24 inches long.

2. Place one base on a level surface, as shown in figure 1.

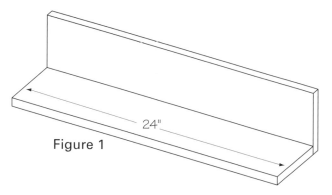

24"

Figure 1

3. Place the second base on edge against one edge of the first base, as shown in figure 1. Apply glue to the meeting surfaces, and screw through the second base into the edge of the first base. Use 1⅝-inch screws spaced about every 4 inches.

4. Label the second base "top." Label the first base "bottom." These labels do not necessarily indicate the top and bottom of the molding to be cut, as that will depend on where the molding will be installed. We'll use the labels for the rest of the construction steps.

5. Use a combination square to mark a 45-degree angle on the top surface of the bottom of the guide. Square a line up the face of the top from the end of the angled line. Finally, mark another 45-degree angle on the edge of the top of the guide, starting at the vertical line, as shown in figure 2.

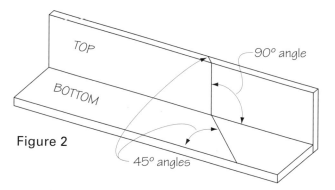

TOP

BOTTOM

90° angle

45° angles

Figure 2

6. Use a backsaw to cut through the top and into (but not through) the bottom.

7. Repeat steps five and six to mark and cut an mirror-image 45-degree angle, as shown in figure 3.

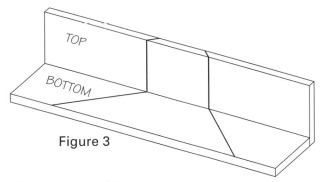

Figure 3

To cut crown molding

1. Place the coved edge (the edge that will be on the "inside" of the miter) of the crown molding against the "top" of the guide, as shown in figure 4. Match your mark to the appropriate kerf in the top of the guide. Nail through the crown molding into the guide, using two small finishing nails on each side of the molding. This will keep the molding from shifting during the cutting process. Depending on the molding you are mitering, spring clamps may work, too.

2. Then follow the kerf in the guide to saw through the crown molding to produce a 45-degree miter.

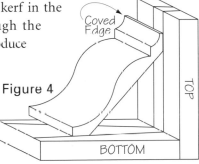

Figure 4

BEVEL

A bevel is also an angular cut, but it refers to an angle cut along the length of a board, rather than across the width as in a miter.

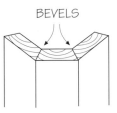

BEVELS

DADO

A dado is a groove cut in the face of one board to accommodate the thickness of another board. It can be cut with a hand saw and chisel, with a router, or with a dado set on a table saw.

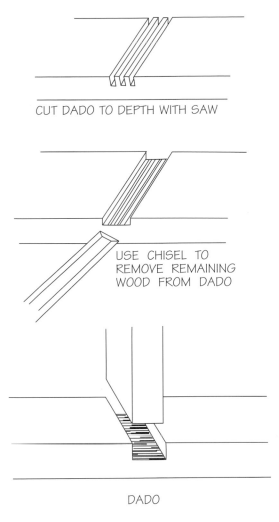

CUT DADO TO DEPTH WITH SAW

USE CHISEL TO REMOVE REMAINING WOOD FROM DADO

DADO

No matter what kind of joint you're making, it is advisable to use both glue and fasteners (nails or screws) whenever possible. The only exception, when you may want to omit the glue, is on joints that you wish to disassemble at a later time.

Particularly if you are a beginner, you may wish to dry-fit your project. This means that you can preassemble portions of the project without glue to make certain that all of the pieces were cut correctly and fit together tightly. You can use clamps to hold the pieces together temporarily or simply hammer small nails into the surface just far enough to hold them in place. Leave a large portion of the nail head above the surface, so the nail will be easy to remove at a later date. Check the fit and trim or adjust the pieces as necessary. Then remove the clamps and/or nails, apply glue, and reassemble the pieces.

Sanding

Of course, any project may be sanded by hand. An inexpensive plastic sanding block will do the job of sanding a level surface just fine. You can even wrap a block of wood with a piece of sandpaper. If you need to sand moldings or curves, try wrapping a pencil or other appropriately sized object with sandpaper.

The amount of sanding that you do on each project depends in a large part on the intended use of the project and on what kind of finish you plan to use. Obviously, if you prefer a rustic look for your project, it need not be sanded completely smooth. However, a rustic chair requires more sanding than a rustic table. Someone will be sitting on it.

An orbital sander does a good job of beginning the sanding process, but it may leave circular marks that must be subsequently sanded out by hand.

A finishing sander is probably the most practical power sander for furniture projects. It has the ability to smooth the surface quickly, and it does not leave circular marks.

A belt sander is often used for large jobs. It sands quickly, but it is difficult to control on softwood such as pine. Because of its power, a belt sander can easily gouge softwood or, if you don't watch carefully, it can remove more of the wood than you wish.

No matter what tool you use, begin sanding with coarse grit and gradually progress to sandpaper with a fine grit. An open-coat aluminum oxide paper is best for sanding both softwoods and hardwoods. Some brands offer "no-load" or "stearated" coatings which reduce the amount of dust clogging the grit. And throw that sandpaper away as soon as it quits working! There's no sense prolonging the job to save a few cents.

SANDING TOOLS. Clockwise from top: belt sander, orbital sander, sanding block from scrap wood, assortment of sandpaper, tack cloth for dust removal, and finishing sansder

ROUTER AND DRILL. Left: router and bits, including rabbet, flush trim, round-over, and straight bits. Right: battery-operated drill with drill bits (top), and counter-sink pilot bit (center). Bottom-right: assortment of wood plugs (bungs) and plug cutter

MATERIALS

Adhesives

The most widely used glue for woodworking is aliphatic resin. It is marketed almost everywhere under names such as "wood glue" or "carpenter's glue."

Don't overdo the amount of glue you use. If too much is applied, the glue will squeeze out of the joint and drip all over your project when pressure is applied. Apply just a small ribbon of glue down the center of one surface and then rub the adjoining surface against the ribbon to distribute the glue evenly. Your objective is to coat both surfaces with a uniform, thin coating. If you do encounter drips, wipe them off quickly with a damp cloth. It's easy to do at that moment but, if you let the glue dry, it is difficult to remove. If it dries, it will have to be sanded off, since it will not accept most stains and will always show up as a different color, even under a clear finish.

Fasteners

NAILS

Although there are many different types of nails (common, large flathead, duplex head, oval head, etc.), the one most commonly used in woodworking is the finish nail. It has a much smaller head than the common nail, making it easy to recess below the surface of the wood (countersinking the nail). The small hole remaining on the surface is easily concealed with wood filler.

Nail sizes are designated by "penny" (abbreviated as "d"). Penny size directly corresponds to length, although the diameter is larger for longer nails. They range in length from 1 inch to 6 inches. To determine the penny size of a particular nail length, the following method works well for lengths up to 3 inches (10d). Take the length of the nail you need, subtract ½ inch and multiply by 4. For example, if you need a 2½-inch nail, subtract ½ inch, leaving 2. Multiply by 4. What you need is an 8-penny nail (8d). Some of the more commonly used sizes of nails are listed in the table below.

Penny Size	Length (in inches)	Penny Size	Length (in inches)	Penny Size	Length (in inches)
2d	1	6d	2	10d	3
3d	1¼	7d	2¼	12d	3¼
4d	1½	8d	2½	16d	3½
5d	1¾	9d	2¾	20d	4

As a general rule, when joining two pieces of wood together, use a nail length that will provide the greatest amount of holding power without penetrating the opposite surface. For example, if you are joining two 1 x 4s, each piece of wood is ¾ inches thick—a total of 1½ inches of wood. To maximize your holding power, you should choose a 1¼-inch (3d) nail.

Nails driven in at an angle provide more holding power than those that are driven straight into the work. Toenailing refers to the process of driving a nail into the wood at an extreme angle to secure two pieces together.

The most difficult part of toenailing comes when the nail is nearly into the wood and only the head and a bit of the shank are visible. To avoid making hammer marks on your wood, hammer the nail into the piece until the head is still slightly above the surface. Then use a nail set to finish the job and countersink the nail.

In fact, the best way to prevent hammer marks on all of your work is to use a nail set. The trick to using a nail set effectively is to hold it in the proper manner. It should be steadied with the hand by gripping it firmly with all four fingers and your thumb. Rest your little finger on the surface of the wood for added stability.

If you are working with hardwood, a very narrow piece of softwood, or any wood that has a tendency to split when you nail into it, it is wise to predrill the nail hole. Choose a drill bit that is just barely smaller than the diameter of the nail and drill a pilot hole about two-thirds the length of the nail.

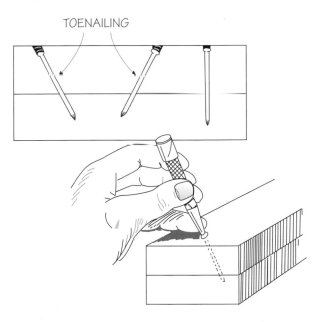

TOENAILING

FASTENERS. An assortment of finishing nails and drywall screws

BRADS

Wire brads are used for attaching trim or for very small projects. They are just a smaller and thinner version of finish nails. They are designated in length in inches and wire gauge numbers from 11 to 20. The lower the gauge number, the larger the diameter.

STAPLES AND STAPLE GUNS

Staples are another variety of light-duty fastener. They are often used to attach fabric to wood. A staple gun is a worthwhile investment and a handy piece of equipment to have around the house. Staple guns are available in many sizes and prices. Although electric models are available and nice to have, a heavy-duty hand staple gun will probably be all that you need initially. It is worthwhile to purchase staples in a variety of lengths to accommodate different thicknesses of material.

SCREWS

The advantages of screws over nails are their holding power and the fact that (when used without glue) they can be removed easily at a later date. Their disadvantage is that they are not as easy to insert.

As with nails, there are many kinds of screws. The one most often used in woodworking is a flathead Phillips screw. As the name implies, it has a flat head that can be countersunk below the surface. It is most often labeled as a "drywall screw" and can be driven with a power drill.

Screws are designated by length and diameter. In general, as with nails, you want to use the longest screw possible that won't penetrate the opposite surface. The diameter of a screw is described by its gauge number. Common sizes range from #2 to #16, with larger diameters having higher gauge numbers. The screws used in the projects in this book range from #6 to #10.

When you are working on very soft wood it is possible to countersink a screw simply by driving it with a power drill. However, the resulting surface hole may be covered only by using wood filler. An alternate method is to predrill the screw hole and insert a wood plug over the top of the countersunk screw head.

This predrilling is normally a two step operation. First drill the larger, countersunk portion at a diameter just slightly larger than the diameter of the screw head and deep enough to accomodate it. If you will be filling the hole with a wood plug, the diameter of the plug determines the size of the countersinking bit. Then drill the pilot hole in the center of the larger hole, using a drill bit the same diameter as the solid portion of the screw (minus the threads). If you use the same size screws on a regular basis, you may wish to invest in a combination pilot/countersink bit for your drill, which will perform both operations at the same time.

You can purchase wood plugs or you can cut your own. It is easy to slice a wooden dowel into many wood plugs. The only disadvantage to this plug is that it will show the end grain and will be visible if you stain the wood. The alternative is to cut your own plugs using a plug cutter, but that method requires a drill press.

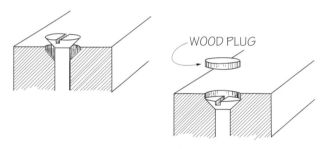

Screws can be inserted at an angle, the same way that nails are, to toenail two pieces of wood together. After some practice, you will be able to start a screw at any angle with very little or no effort. If you find it difficult, simply use a drill or a screw starter to begin your screw hole.

Although you don't want to add so many screws to your project that the metal outweighs the wood, I am not stingy with them. If there is the slightest chance that the joint could be shaky, I add a couple of extra screws. Remember that the project you are making will probably be subjected to several moves over the course of the years—either to a different room or a different house—which will place additional strain on the joints.

Lumber

The two basic classifications of wood are softwood and hardwood. As the name implies, softwood is usually softer and therefore easier to work with than hardwood. It is also usually less expensive. Because of this, softwood is often a good choice for beginning woodworkers. We built all of the projects in this book with softwood but, of course, they can be built with hardwood. We have specified pine in the instructions, but use whatever softwood is most plentiful (and least expensive) in your area. Softwood is cut from coniferous trees (evergreens) such as pine, redwood, and cedar. Hardwood comes from deciduous trees such as maple, cherry, and walnut, which shed their leaves each year.

SOFTWOOD

Softwood is sold in most building supply stores in dimensional sizes—1 x 4s, 2 x 4s, etc. And it is sold in specific lengths at two-foot intervals: you can buy a 1 x 4 x 6, or a 1 x 4 x 8, or a 1 x 4 x 10, and so forth. This would seem to make it simple. And it would be if a 1 x 4 were actually 1 inch thick and 4 inches wide. But such is not the case. Apparently the sawmills, lumberyards, and building supply stores have conspired in a huge plot to confuse us, because a 1 x 4 is actually ¾ inch thick and 3½ inches wide. There is a reason for this. When the board was sawn from a log, it was 1 inch thick and 4 inches wide. But when it is surfaced on all four sides, its actual dimensions are less. Listed below are the nominal sizes and the actual dimensions:

Nominal Size	Actual Dimensions	Nominal Size	Actual Dimensions
1 x 2	¾" x 1½"	2 x 6	1½" x 5½"
1 x 3	¾" x 2½"	2 x 8	1½" x 7¼"
1 x 4	¾" x 3½"	2 x 10	1½" x 9¼"
1 x 6	¾" x 5½"	2 x 12	1½" x 11¼"
1 x 8	¾" x 7¼"	4 x 4	3½" x 3½"
1 x 10	¾" x 9¼"	4 x 6	3½" x 5½"
1 x 12	¾" x 11¼"	6 x 6	5½" x 5½"
2 x 2	1½" x 1½"	8 x 8	7½" x 7½"
2 x 4	1½" x 3½"		

Softwood is also graded according to its quality. As with anything else, the better the quality, the higher the price. Don't buy a better quality than you need for the project you are building. A few imperfections may even make your project look more rustic (if that is the look you are after). The softwood grades are as follows:

Common Grades:

NO. 1 COMMON—Contains small knots and a few imperfections, but should have no knotholes.

NO. 2 COMMON—Free of knotholes, but contains some knots.

NO. 3 COMMON—Contains larger knots and small knotholes.

NO. 4 COMMON—Used for construction only. Contains large knotholes.

NO. 5 COMMON—Lowest grade of lumber. Used only when strength and appearance are not necessary.

Select Grades:

B AND BETTER (OR 1 AND 2 CLEAR)—The best and most expensive grades used for the finest furniture projects.

C SELECT—May have a few small blemishes.

D SELECT—The lowest quality of the better board grades. It has imperfections that can be concealed with paint.

The clear boards (those that are nearly free of imperfections) come from the outer section of the tree. The center section (heartwood) contains more knots and other flaws.

Consider the type of finish that you want to apply to the completed project. If you plan to stain the finished piece, pay particular attention to the grain of the wood that you are buying and choose boards that have fewer imperfections and similar grain patterns.

If you are going to paint the finished piece, you can purchase a lower grade of wood and cover the defects with wood filler and paint.

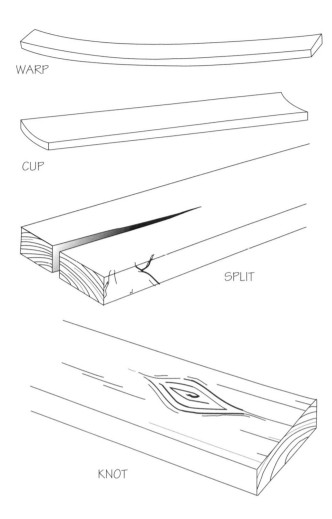

WARP

CUP

SPLIT

KNOT

INSPECTING YOUR LUMBER

No matter what grade you purchase, you should inspect each and every board for defects and imperfections. A little extra inspection time in the store will prove well worth the effort by saving you hours of frustration later. Some places will not allow you to hand-select individual boards—take your business elsewhere. While it is possible (but extremely time-consuming) to correct some defects in wood, it is simply easier to purchase blemish-free boards in the first place. There is no point in buying wood that is unusable, no matter how cheap the price.

Many large building supply stores purchase their wood from different suppliers, and that means that, even in the same bin at the same store, the board widths may vary slightly. On the surface (no pun intended), that may not seem like a big deal. But even a difference of $\frac{1}{64}$ of an inch in width between two boards may mean that your project will not fit together correctly. So when you purchase wood for a specific project, place the boards together to make certain that they are all exactly the same width.

While you are checking, examine the board for warpage, cupping, and twist. Warpage is a curve along the length of the board, while cupping occurs across the width of the board. Twist refers to just what you think. All of these curved surfaces indicate interior stresses in the plank. They don't go away by themselves. If you will be cutting only very short pieces of wood and the warpage is very slight, it probably will not affect your finished project. But if you need longer lengths, search until you find boards that are straight along the entire length. A good method to check for warping or cupping before you buy is to place one end of the board on the floor and look down its length. Then turn the board and look down the edge. Your own eye is the best test.

Also check for knots. Small, tight knots are usually okay—especially for furniture that you plan to paint. But large knots may become a problem, as they are tough to cut through and also may fall out, leaving you with an unattractive hole in your finished project. Some imperfections can simply be eliminated. If a board is otherwise acceptable but has a knothole on the end, it is easy enough to simply cut it off. But be sure to purchase extra material to compensate for the loss.

Avoid buying boards that contain splits. Splits have a nasty habit of growing lengthwise, ultimately resulting in two narrow and unusable boards. If the split occurs only at one end, you can cut it off but, again, allow extra material for the waste.

When you begin cutting pieces for your project, always cut the longest pieces first. That way, if you inadvertently miscut a piece you can use that board to cut the short pieces for the project.

Also reexamine each board before you cut it. If you need a 5-foot piece from a 6-foot plank, eliminate the end that has the most defects. During assembly, examine each piece again, and use the best side of each board where it will be seen. Following these steps will save a lot of time in filling and sanding, and will also give you a better-looking finished project.

For purposes of clarity, this book refers to each surface of a board by a specific name. The broadest part of the board is called a face, and the narrow surface along the length of the board is an edge. The ends, as the name suggests, are the smallest surfaces on the extremities of each board.

Please read through the instructions and cutting list for your project before shopping for materials. Each materials list specifies the total number of linear feet of a particular wood required to make the project. So if the total linear feet required is 40 feet, you can purchase five 8-foot lengths, four 10-foot lengths, and so on. When you arrive at the lumberyard or store you may find that the 8-foot lengths of wood are of lesser quality than the 6-foot lengths. You could then buy seven 6-foot lengths and have a little left over, but you must first check to make certain that no single piece required by the project is over 6 feet long.

It is also wise to keep transportation abilities in mind. If you own (or can borrow) a pickup truck to transport your materials, board lengths are not a factor. But it's pretty difficult to get a 12-foot length of wood into a Corvette for the trip home. Most building supply stores will be happy to give you one free cut on an individual piece of lumber, but some charge a fee.

Unless you have chosen a very expensive wood with which to build your project, it makes sense to slightly overbuy your materials. That way, if you do make a mistake, you have a "reserve" board to bail you out. Returning to the store for just one more board is frustrating, time-consuming, and (depending upon how far you drive) sometimes more expensive than if you had purchased an extra one on the original trip. We have built some overage into the materials list to accommodate squaring the piece and allowing for the width of saw cuts.

HARDWOOD

You can also use hardwood to build any of the projects in this book. Hardwood, as the name implies, will resist dents and scratches much better than softwood. The downside is that it is more difficult to work with, and it is more expensive.

If you decide to use a hardwood for your project, it will take some calculating on your part, since hardwood is normally sold in random widths and lengths. Each board is cut from the log as wide and as long as possible. Consequently, hardwood is sold by a measure called the board foot. A board foot represents a piece of lumber 1 inch thick, 12 inches wide, and 1 foot long. Hardwood thicknesses are measured in quarter inches. The standard thicknesses are 4/4, 5/4, 6/4, and 8/4 (pronounced "four-quarter," "five-quarter," etc., not "four-fourths"). A 4/4 cherry plank 6 inches wide and 10 feet long is 5 board feet (BF). Board foot measurement generally indicates that the lumber is "rough," not surfaced. Even if the boards you buy have been thickness-planed to 3/4 inch, you pay for 4/4 lumber, of course.

Plywood

As you might guess, plywood is made from several plies of wood that are glued together with the grain of each successive layer placed at right angles to the last. It is sold in sheets measuring 4 feet by 8 feet. In some supply stores you can also purchase half-sheets measuring 4 feet by 4 feet. Plywood comes in standard thicknesses of $\frac{1}{8}$, $\frac{1}{4}$, $\frac{3}{8}$, $\frac{1}{2}$, $\frac{5}{8}$, and $\frac{3}{4}$ inch.

There are two principal kinds of plywood: veneer-core and lumber-core. Lumber-core is the higher quality material: its edges can be worked as you would work solid wood. The exposed cut edges of veneer-core plywood must be either filled or covered because they are unsightly.

Plywood is also graded according to the quality of the outer veneer. The grades are "A" through "D," with "A" representing the best quality. A piece of plywood has two designations, one for each face. For example, an "A-D" piece has one veneered surface that is "A" quality and one that is "D" quality. Plywood also comes designated "interior" or "exterior." The only difference between these grades is the glue used to hold the plies together.

Just as you inspected planks for warpage and cupping, watch out for plywood sheets that twist. Plywood twist is caused by improper manufacturing and will not disappear. Twisted plywood is suitable only for underlayment or roof decking, not for furniture.

Finishes

The finish that you apply to your finished project is extremely important. Your choice of finish and the care with which you apply it will make a considerable difference in the look of your finished project. The better the finish, the longer you will be enjoying your handiwork.

There are hundreds of different products on the market, but the first choice is whether to stain, paint, or simply seal your project. The advantages and disadvantages of each choice are as follows:

PAINT

Paint will cover a multitude of flaws. It is possible to take wood that is not at all attractive in appearance, apply a flawless coat of paint, and produce an extremely good-looking piece of furniture. The disadvantage is that the wood must be thoroughly filled, sanded, and primed, all of which takes time and effort. Then it must be given two coats of paint, and at least one coat of sealer should be applied.

When shopping for paint, look for special characteristics that protect against local weather problems. For example, here in Florida, many paints are treated with special additives that protect against mildew, which occurs in our high humidity. Also look to see how long the paint is warranted.

Most professionals swear by very expensive hog bristle brushes. We use them only when there is absolutely no choice in the matter. We much prefer sponge brushes,

which are extremely cheap and can be thrown in the trash after use. Look for the ones that have a smooth surface like a cosmetic sponge and a wooden handle. If you are interrupted in midcoat and the sponge brush is not yet ready for tossing, just pop your brush into an airtight sandwich bag. You can leave it there for a day or so and it will still be pliable and ready to use.

STAIN

Stains used to come in brown or brown. True, there were gray-browns and yellow-browns and red-browns—but they were all brown. And it used to be very difficult to apply them evenly. How times have changed! These days stains come in a terrific variety of colors, from the palest white to the darkest black. And they also range from extremely translucent to nearly opaque. They have the additional advantage of being extremely easy to apply, usually requiring only one coat. Although most manufacturers recommend that you apply their product with a brush, I have found that a plain old rag gives a very smooth and even appearance to most stains. (I don't guarantee best results with every type of stain, so I recommend you try it either on a scrap piece of wood or on a surface that will not show before attacking the entire project with my method.)

FINISHING MATERIALS. Clockwise from left: water-based wood filler and putty knife; assortment of finishes and stains; disposable foam brushes; and a natural bristle brush

SAFETY

WORKING WITH POWER TOOLS CAN BE DANGEROUS. In a fight with a power saw, you will be the loser. And losing is extremely painful. I know many woodworkers, and many of them have missing digits. If that sounds scary, that's good. Read the instructions that are provided with every tool and follow them religiously. Again, we stress that the instructions in this book are written for the beginner using hand tools and must be altered when using power tools. Never attempt a maneuver that is not appropriate to the power tool you are using. Misuse of power tool equipment can lead to serious injury to yourself or damage to the tool.

Never take your eyes off the work. Always concentrate on what you are doing and take the necessary safety precautions. Just one moment of lost concentration or not following the safety rules can result in frightful consequences. Develop the habit of avoiding the path of the saw—do not stand directly behind it or directly in front of it. Power saws can flip a piece of wood back at you with incredible force.

Always wear safety goggles when working with wood. Avoiding just one splinter aimed at your eye makes this practice worth your while. A dust mask is a prudent accessory when working with wood. Sawdust can be very irritating to your lungs. You can choose from a number of different types, from a simple paper mask to those with replaceable filters.

If you use power tools—especially circular saws, which can be quite loud—a pair of ear plugs or protectors is a good investment. Prolonged exposure to loud noise can have harmful effects on your hearing.

Using protective gear also provides a hidden safety benefit: when you insulate yourself from the irritating aspects of woodworking, you can concentrate better on doing a good job.

THE PROJECTS

So you've looked through the book and already decided which project you want to build first. Before you jump in the car for your trip to the building supply store, slow yourself down long enough to read this section. We've included just the basic information on how the instructions are organized and about the special tips that will save you money and effort.

Materials and Supplies

The materials list for each project specifies in linear feet the amount of wood you will need. Where we have specified pine, we simply mean a decent grade of dimensional lumber. By all means, if fir is more available, use it. We have allowed a slight overage in the number of feet required to square the ends of each board and to cover waste, but it is always prudent to overbuy slightly. A trip back to the store to buy "just one more 2 x 4" is frustrating at best.

For purposes of clarity in the project instructions, each board surface has been named. The broadest part of the board is called its face, and the narrow surface along the length is its edge. The ends, obviously, are the smallest surfaces at each end of the board.

Hardware

We have also specified the number of nails, screws, etc. that you will need, in addition to other hardware for the project you have chosen. We recognize that you will purchase nails and screws by the box, and will not actually buy "12 nails," but our total will give you a reference amount. Again, it is always prudent to have extra supplies.

Tools and Techniques

Each project lists any special tools that you may not have and techniques that you may need to learn. Check the list before you go shopping. If it calls for a staple gun and you don't own one, now is the time to decide whether to purchase a staple gun or select a different project. In the same way, if a project calls for dadoes and you aren't familiar with the term, read through that portion of "Tools, Techniques, and Materials," and practice the maneuver before you begin the project.

If you are an advanced woodworker who possesses large stationary power tools, read through the project instructions before beginning, since you will probably want to modify the procedures to accommodate your advanced knowledge and tools. Bear in mind that these instructions are written for very basic tools, and some techniques may need to be "translated" in order to use your tools safely. For instance, a dado may be cut by hand, on a table saw, or with a router, but each of these methods requires a different setup and specific knowledge of the tools involved. Know the capabilities of your tools, and don't exceed them.

Cutting List

The cutting list is an exact guide for cutting each piece of wood for your project. Don't cut all the pieces right away. The instructions will walk you through cutting each piece as it is required in the building process. Do, however, read through the cutting list before you shop for your materials. If your project calls for an eight-foot length, you shouldn't purchase all of your 1 x 4s in 6-foot lengths.

Inspect each piece of wood before you buy it. Avoid buying wood that is warped, twisted, or cupped. The easiest way to check a board is to place one end on the floor and look down the length of its face. Then turn the board and look down its edge. Any unwanted curves will be obvious immediately.

Also keep in mind that you will have to transport the lumber back home. If your project requires 10-foot lengths of wood, and you drive a small car, call a friend to borrow a pickup truck or have the wood delivered.

Consider how you want to finish the surface of your project. Lower grades of wood can be used if you plan to paint, because wood filler and paint will cover many imperfections. On the other hand, if you plan to stain the wood, choose a better grade and pick boards with similar grain patterns.

When it's time to start cutting, cut the longest project pieces first. If you miscut, you'll still have plenty of wood to cut another piece, and you can use the miscut board for a shorter piece. Pay some attention, too, to the size of the "waste" piece from each board. Try to produce cutoffs that can be used for other pieces in the project.

One Final Tip

An overall "game plan" is essential in woodworking. The more you understand about the project you are going to make and how the pieces fit together, the smoother the work will go. Woodworking is a step-by-step process, in which one step must be completed before the next one is begun. It is also a process in which $1/64$ of an inch can make a difference. If you understand where the next piece goes and cut it just before you use it, you can check to make sure that your assembly is truly accurate and adjust for any small inaccuracies.

No woodworker, regardless of his or her experience level, avoids making mistakes. But if you look at your slip-ups as part of the learning process and file them under "things not to do again," then your woodworking becomes a constantly evolving experience. If you slip up several times in a row, take a break and come back to it. Your projects will turn out better, and you will be a safer and more satisfied woodworker.

Telephone Table

We have a kitchen wall phone, but had nowhere to sit and write. This telephone table serves the purpose nicely. It's a snap to make and serves as a very convenient area for phone books, notepads, and writing instruments.

Materials

- 7 linear feet of 1 x 6 pine
- 2 linear feet of 1 x 12 pine
- 5 linear feet of 3" chair rail molding
- 2 newel posts*

Hardware

- 20 1" (2d) finish nails
- 24 1½" screws
- 12 2½" screws

Cutting List

Code	Description	Qty.	Materials	Dimensions
A	Top	1	1 x 12 pine	24" long
B	Front/Back	2	1 x 6 pine	24" long
C	Side	2	1 x 6 pine	12¾" long
D	Leg	2	newel posts*	39" long
E	Trim	3	3-inch chair rail molding	cut to fit

✳ Notes on Materials

We purchased newel posts at a building supply store, turned them upside down, and used them for the legs. If you can't find the exact kind we used, you can substitute a 4 x 4 and attach a fence-post finial on the end–or simply use a 4 x 4 by itself. Just make certain that the total length of the leg is 39 inches.

MAKING THE TABLE TOP

1. Cut one top (A) from 1 x 12 pine, measuring 24 inches long.

2. Cut two front/backs (B) from 1 x 6 pine, each measuring 24 inches long.

3. Cut two sides (C) from 1 x 6 pine, each measuring 12¾ inches long.

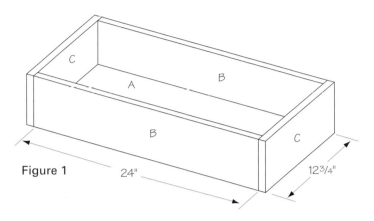

Figure 1   24"   12¾"

4. Place the top (A) on a level surface. Place the two front/backs (B) on edge on either side of the top (A), matching the 24-inch-long sides, as shown in figure 1. Apply glue to the edges of the top (A), and screw through the front/backs (B) into the edges of the top (A), using six evenly spaced 1½-inch screws on each joint.

5. Place the two sides (C) over the ends of the two front/backs (B), as shown in figure 2. Screw through the sides (C) into the ends of the front/backs (B) and into the ends of the top (A), using three 1½-inch screws on each joint.

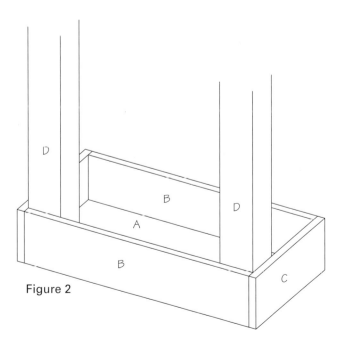

Figure 2

ADDING THE LEGS

6. Trim the two legs (D) to 39 inches long.

7. Place the legs (D) inside the table assembly, as shown in figure 2. Note that both legs (D) are attached to the same front (B). Apply glue to the meeting surfaces, and screw through the front (B) and sides (C) into the legs (D), using two 2½-inch screws on each joint. After driving each screw, use a try square to make sure that the legs (D) remain at right angles to both front (A) and side (C). Also screw through the top (A) into the legs (D), using two 2½-inch screws on each leg (D).

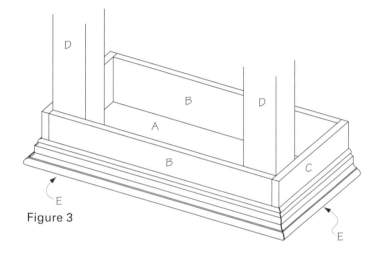

Figure 3

FINISHING

8. Measure carefully, and cut the outer trim (D) from 3-inch-wide molding, as shown in figure 3, mitering the molding at each of the corners. Do not attach molding to the back of the telephone table, as the back will be attached to a wall. Apply glue to the meeting surfaces, and nail through the outer trim (D) into the front and sides (B and C). Use 1-inch (2d) finish nails spaced about every 4 inches.

9. Fill any screw holes or imperfections in the wood with wood filler.

10. Thoroughly sand the telephone table.

11. Stain or paint the table the color of your choice. Since we use it in our kitchen, we chose a bright white paint to coordinate with our other kitchen items.

12. Use molly bolts or other appropriate hardware to secure the finished table to a wall.

what do you need?

When we walked into this tiny, neglected kitchen the first time, Mark and I both turned green—not unlike the avocado shade that covered every surface in that depressing room. First, we attacked the cosmetic problems. We selected a lively wallpaper pattern to take your eye away from the mismatched appliances, and we used white paint to brighten the dark wood cabinets.

Then we began thinking of things we could build to make the kitchen function smoothly. We decided that we needed three pieces of furniture: a hutch for additional storage, an island to provide an additional work surface, and a telephone table to serve as a kitchen desk. Finally, we painted all of our new furniture white to match the cabinets.

China Hutch

This charming hutch brightens our kitchen and provides space for cookbooks, coffee cups, and pasta jars. The lower cabinet is large enough to store all those oversized containers that won't fit anywhere else.

china hutch

Materials List

- 4 linear feet of 1 x 2 pine
- 48 linear feet of 1 x 4 pine
- 20 linear feet of 1 x 6 pine
- 18 linear feet of 1 x 12 pine
- 1½ sheets (4' x 8') of ¼" beaded plywood
- 6 linear feet of 4"-wide crown molding

Hardware

- 44 ¾" wire brads
- 18 1" (2d) finish nails
- 110 1¼" (3d) finish nails
- 98 1½" wood screws
- 12 2" wood screws
- 2 molly bolts
- 4 cabinet hinges
- 2 door pulls
- 2 cabinet catches

Special Tools and Techniques

- Pipe clamps
- Miters

Cutting List

Code	Description	Qty.	Materials	Dimensions
A	Cabinet Top/Bottom	2	1 x 12 pine	48" long
B	Cabinet Sides	2	1 x 12 pine	34½" long
C	Cabinet Shelf	1	1 x 12 pine	46½" long
D	Cabinet Top/ Bottom Trim	2	1 x 4 pine	48" long
E	Cabinet Side Trim	2	1 x 4 pine	29" long
F	Reinforcing Blocks	4	1 x 2 pine	2½" long
G	Cabinet Back	1	¼" plywood	36" x 48"
H	Top/Bottom Door Trim	4	1 x 4 pine	21½" long
I	Side Door Trims	4	1 x 4 pine	24" long
J	Door Panel	2	¼" plywood	19" x 28½"

Cutting List, continued

Code	Description	Qty.	Materials	Dimensions
K	Hutch Top	1	1 x 6 pine	48" long
L	Hutch Side	2	1 x 6 pine	41½" long
M	Hutch Shelf	2	1 x 6 pine	46½" long
N	Hutch Side Trim	2	1 x 4 pine	42¼" long
O	Hutch Top Trim	1	1 x 4 pine	41" long
P	Hutch Shelf Trim	2	1 x 4 pine	41" long
Q	Reinforcing Blocks	6	1 x 2 pine	2½" long
R	Hutch Back	1	¼" plywood	48" x 42¼"

CONSTRUCTING THE LOWER CABINET

1. Cut two cabinet top/bottoms (A) from 1 x 12 pine, each measuring 48 inches long.

2. Cut two cabinet sides (B) from 1 x 12 pine, each measuring 34½ inches long.

3. Place the cabinet top/bottoms (A) parallel to each other and 34½ inches apart. Fit the two cabinet sides (B) between the two cabinet top/bottoms to form a rectangle measuring 36 x 48 inches, as shown in figure 1. Screw through the cabinet top/bottoms (A) into the ends of the cabinet sides (B). Use three 1½-inch screws on each of the joints.

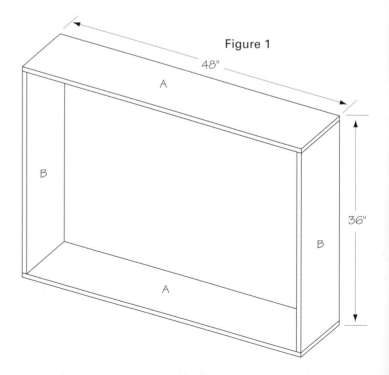

Figure 1

4. Cut one cabinet shelf (C) from 1 x 12 pine, measuring 46½ inches long.

5. Center the cabinet shelf (C) between the two cabinet top/bottoms (A), as shown in figure 2. Screw through the cabinet sides (B) into the ends of the cabinet shelf (C), using three 1½-inch screws on each joint.

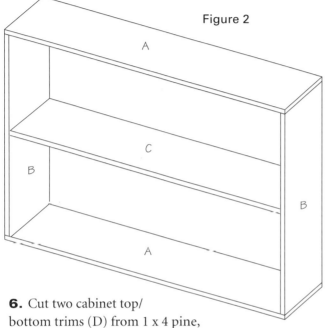

Figure 2

6. Cut two cabinet top/ bottom trims (D) from 1 x 4 pine, each measuring 48 inches long.

7. Apply glue to the meeting surfaces, and attach one cabinet top/bottom trim (D) to the front edge of a cabinet top/bottom (A), as shown in figure 3. Screw through the cabinet top/bottom trim (D) into the edge of the cabinet top/bottom (A), using 1½-inch-long screws spaced approximately every 6 inches.

8. Repeat step 7 to attach the remaining cabinet top/bottom trim (D) to the front edge of the remaining cabinet top/bottom (A).

9. Cut two cabinet side trims (E) from 1 x 4 pine, each measuring 29 inches long.

10. Apply glue to the edge of one cabinet side (B), and attach one cabinet side trim (E) to the edge of one cabinet side (B), as shown in figure 3. Use 1½-inch screws and space them approximately 6 inches apart.

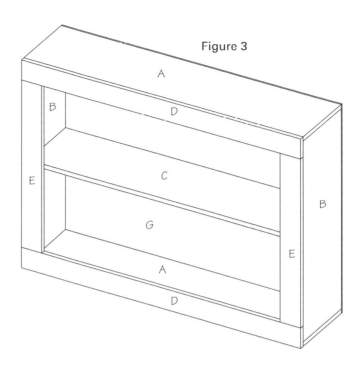

Figure 3

11. Repeat step 10 to attach the remaining cabinet side trim (E) to the remaining cabinet side (B).

12. Cut four reinforcing blocks (F) from 1 x 2 pine, each measuring 2½ inches long.

13. Place the cabinet trim side down and fit one reinforcing block (F) inside the upper left corner of the cabinet across the joint between the cabinet top/bottom trim (D) and the cabinet side trim (E). Apply glue to the reinforcing block (F), and nail it over the joint, placing one 1¼-inch (3d) finish nail on each side of the joint.

14. Repeat step 13 three more times to attach the remaining three reinforcing blocks (F) over the remaining three joints in the corners of the cabinet.

15. Cut one cabinet back (G) from ¼-inch plywood, measuring 36 x 48 inches.

16. Fit the cabinet back (G) over the back of the cabinet, as shown in figure 3. Apply glue to the meeting surfaces, and nail through the cabinet back (G) into the edges of the top/bottoms (A), sides (B), and shelf (C), using 1¼-inch (3d) finish nails spaced about 5 inches apart.

MAKING THE CABINET DOORS

17. Cut four top/bottom door trims (H) from 1 x 4 pine, each measuring 21½ inches long.

18. Cut four side door trims (I) from 1 x 4 pine, each measuring 24 inches long.

19. Cut two door panels (J) from ¼-inch-thick plywood, measuring 19 x 28½ inches.

20. Place two top/bottom door trims (H) face down, parallel to each other, and 24 inches apart.

21. Fit two side door trims (I) face down between the two top/bottom door trims, as shown in figure 4.

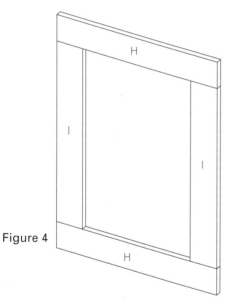

Figure 4

22. Center a door panel (J) over the door trims. There should be a 1¼-inch border of trim on all sides of the door panel (J). Apply glue to the meeting surfaces, and nail through the door panel into the each of the four trim pieces (H and I) using ¾-inch brads, placed about every 4 inches.

23. Repeat steps 20, 21, and 22 using the remaining two top/bottom door trims (H), the two side door trims (I), and door panel (J).

24. The next step is optional. We routed both the inside and outside edges of the front of the assembled door trims (H and I) using a round-over bit.

25. Place the completed cabinet on its back and place the two cabinet doors over the front opening in the cabinet. Allow about ⅛ inch of space between the two doors. Check to make certain that the doors are straight and that they are equidistant from the sides, bottom, and top of the cabinet. Then attach the doors to the cabinet using two hinges on each door. Also install door catches on each of the cabinet doors to make certain that they will stay closed when you shut them.

MAKING THE UPPER HUTCH SECTION

26. Cut one hutch top (K) from 1 x 6 pine, measuring 48 inches long.

27. Cut two hutch sides (L) from 1 x 6 pine, each measuring 41½ inches long.

28. Place the two hutch sides (L) parallel to each other, and 46½ inches apart. Place the hutch top (K) over the ends of the two hutch sides (L), as shown in figure 5. Screw through the hutch top (K) into the ends of the hutch sides (L). Use three 2-inch screws on each joint.

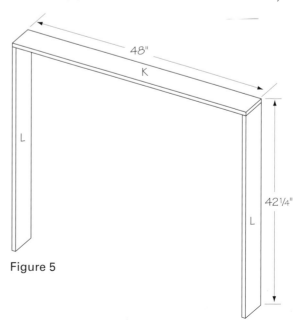

Figure 5

29. Cut two hutch shelves (M) from 1 x 6 pine, each measuring 46½ inches long.

30. Place one hutch shelf (M) between the two hutch sides (L), 13 inches from the hutch top (K), as shown in figure 6. Screw through the hutch sides (L) into the ends of the hutch shelf (M). Use three 1½-inch screws on each of the joints.

31. Place the remaining hutch shelf (M) between the two hutch sides (L), 13 inches from the first hutch shelf (M), as shown in figure 6. Again, screw through the hutch sides (L) into the ends of the hutch shelf (M). Use three 1½-inch screws on each of the joints.

32. Cut two hutch side trims (N) from 1 x 4 pine, each measuring 42¼ inches long.

33. Apply glue to the meeting surfaces, and attach one hutch side trim (N) to the front edge of the hutch top (K) and the hutch side (L), as shown in figure 7. Screw through the hutch side trim (N) into both the hutch top and side (K and L), using 1½-inch screws spaced about every 5 inches.

34. Repeat step 33 to attach the remaining hutch side trim (N) to the opposite hutch side (L) and the hutch top (K).

35. Cut one hutch top trim (O) from 1 x 4 pine, measuring 41 inches long.

36. Apply glue to the meeting surfaces, and attach the hutch top trim (O) to the front edge of the hutch top (K) between the two hutch side trims (N). Screw through the hutch top trim into the edge of the hutch top (K), using 1½-inch screws spaced about every 5 inches.

37. Cut two hutch shelf trims (P) from 1 x 4 pine, each measuring 41 inches long.

38. Apply glue to the meeting surfaces, and attach each of the hutch shelf trims (P) to the front edge of the hutch shelves (M), between the two hutch side trims (N), and flush with the top of the hutch shelves (M). Screw through the hutch shelf trims (P) into the edges of the hutch shelves (M), using 1½-inch screws spaced about every 5 inches.

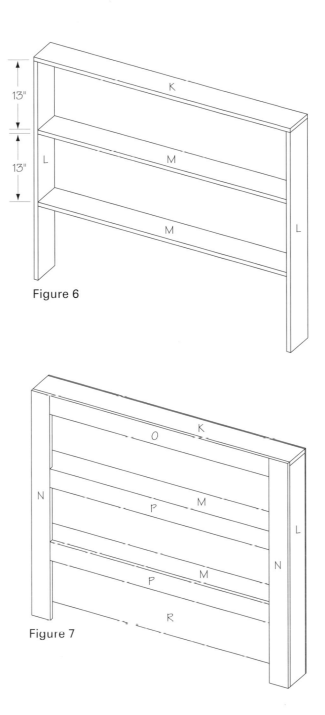

Figure 6

Figure 7

39. Cut six reinforcing blocks (Q) from 1 x 2 pine, each measuring 2½ inches long.

40. Place the hutch assembly trim side down and fit one reinforcing block (Q) inside the upper left corner of the hutch across the joint between the hutch side trim (M) and the hutch top trim (O). Apply glue to the reinforcing block (Q), and nail it over the joint, placing one 1¼-inch (3d) finish nail on each side of the joint.

41. Repeat step 40 five more times to attach the remaining five reinforcing blocks over the remaining joint between the hutch side trim (M) and the hutch top trim (O), and over the four joints between the hutch side trim (M) and the hutch shelf trim (P).

42. Cut one hutch back (R) from ¼-inch plywood, measuring 48 x 42¼ inches.

43. Fit the hutch back (R) over the back of the assembled hutch. Apply glue to the meeting surfaces, and nail through the hutch back (R) into the edges of the hutch top (K), the hutch sides (L), and the hutch shelves (M). Use 1¼-inch (3d) finish nails spaced about every 5 inches.

FINISHING

44. Measure carefully to cut and fit lengths of 4-inch-wide crown molding across the top of the hutch front and sides. Apply glue to the meeting surfaces, and secure the molding with 1-inch (3d) finish nails spaced every 4 inches.

45. Fill any cracks, crevices, or imperfections with wood filler and sand the hutch completely.

46. Paint or stain the finished hutch pieces the color of your choice.

47. You may need a helper for the final assembly. Place the hutch section on top of the cabinet section, aligning the sides and back. Have the helper steady the hutch while you connect the two pieces together. We recommend that you forego any glue so that the hutch can be disassembled in case of a move. Insert two or three 2-inch screws through the cabinet top into the ends of each of the hutch sides to pull the two pieces together.

48. Because of the height of the combined hutch and cabinet and its shallow depth, we recommend that you also secure the hutch to the wall with molly bolts or other appropriate hardware.

I'm in the kitchen...

Face facts! If you are preparing food while guests or family are in the house, chances are good that you'll have an audience. Because we enjoy relaxed entertaining, and especially kitchen company, our kitchen island and telephone table are designed to serve as people perches. A plate of appetizers on the island and self-serve beverages on the telephone table make everyone feel at home while we finish preparing the meal.

As the photograph shows, the island tends to keep guests out of our way while it invites them to stay within range to help chop, mix, or assemble. To bend an old proverb: good islands make great kitchen guests.

Kitchen Island

If you need extra countertop space in your kitchen, this island is your answer. Its tiled top is perfect for meal preparation, and the large shelf on the bottom can be used to store giant pots that simply won't fit in regular kitchen cabinets.

kitchen island

Materials List

- 10 linear feet of 1 x 3 pine
- 25 linear feet of 1 x 4 pine
- 22 linear feet of 1 x 6 pine
- 9 linear feet of 2 x 2 pine
- 2 linear feet of 2 x 6 pine
- 12 linear feet of 4 x 4 pine
- 1 piece of ½-inch exterior plywood, 22" x 40"
- 1 piece of ¾-inch plywood, 22¾" x 40"
- 9½ linear feet of 2½"-wide baseboard molding

Hardware

- 20 1" wood screws
- 24 1¼" wood screws
- 20 1½" wood screws
- 16 2" wood screws
- 8   3" wood screws
- 36 1¼" (3d) finish nails
- 30 2" (6d) finish nails
- 42 2½" (8d) finish nails
- 45 4-inch-square tiles,
  or enough to cover a 21¾" x 39" area*
- Tile grout (small container)
- Tile mastic (small container)
- Grout sealer (small bottle)

Special Tools and Techniques

- 3 or 4 large bar clamps or pipe clamps
- Large chisel
- Trowel
- Rubber-surfaced trowel
- Tile cutter (if necessary)*
- Miters

Cutting List

Code	Description	Qty	Material	Dimensions
A	Table Legs	4	4 x 4 pine	27" long
B	Long Side Rails	2	1 x 6 pine	38" long
C	Short Side Rails	2	1 x 6 pine	20¾" long
D	Corner Supports sides	4	2 x 6 pine	5½" on short
E	Short Bottom Frame	2	1 x 6 pine	28¾" long
F	Long Bottom Frame	2	1 x 6 pine	35" long
G	Long Top Frame	2	1 x 4 pine	46" long
H	Short Top Frame	2	1 x 4 pine	21¾" long
I	Center Top	1	½" plywood	21¾" x 39"
J	Long Trim	2	1 x 3 pine	34½" long
K	Short Trim	2	1 x 3 pine	17¼" long
L	Long Molding	2	2½"-wide molding	34½" long
M	Short Molding	2	2½"-wide molding	17¼" long
N	Long Shelf Support	2	2 x 2 pine	40" long
O	Short Shelf Support	4	2 x 2 pine	2¾" long
P	Bottom Shelf	1	¾" plywood	40" x 22¾"
Q	Long Shelf Trim	2	1 x 4 pine	34½" long
R	Short Shelf Trim	2	1 x 4 pine	17¼" long

❋ Notes on Materials

When choosing the tile for this table, consider that the tile must fit in a specified area. If the tile you like will not fit into the dimensions evenly, you can either alter the dimensions of the island or cut some of the tiles. We suggest that you read through the next section, "Constructing the Island Top," which explains how to make certain that your tiles fit the project. If you opt to trim the tile to fit the island dimensions, you also need a tile cutter. We suggest that you purchase a few extra tiles for this project, as they are breakable. To install the tiles, you need a trowel for spreading the mastic and a rubber-surfaced trowel for applying the grout.

CONSTRUCTING THE ISLAND TOP

The island top consists of a center piece of ½-inch exterior plywood that is framed on all four sides with lengths of 1 x 4 pine. The difference in thickness between the ½-inch plywood and the ¾-inch-thick pine allows for the addition of ceramic tile in the center of the island.

The following instructions are given to fit exactly the tiles that we purchased for the center of the island. It has been our experience that even 4-inch tiles by different manufacturers may vary slightly in dimensions. That slight variation can cause the finished island top to be off by a substantial amount, so before cutting any pieces for this project, we suggest that you make certain that the tiles you have will fit the dimensions we have given. In the event that they do not, you will need to alter the dimensions of the island top pieces to accommodate your own tiles.

To verify your own dimensions, arrange your tiles on your uncut piece of ½-inch exterior plywood. We had five rows of nine tiles each, as shown in figure 1. Measure the outer edges of your tiles, allowing for a border of grout around the outer edges the same width as the space between the tiles.

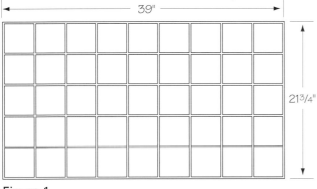

Figure 1

Draw a line around the tiles (including the outer grout allowance), forming a rectangle. Compare the dimensions of your rectangle to the size specified in the instructions for the center top (C). If it deviates from those measurements (21¾ x 39 inches), you must adjust the size of the center plywood, and also the lengths of all of the additional island top pieces (B, C, G, and H).

In order to ensure a flat island top when you are finished, you must also check that the thickness of the plywood plus the thickness of the tile (and any tile mastic that you place under the tile) is equal to the thickness of the 1 x 4 pine that borders the island. The tile we use is just under ¼-inch thick. You can vary the thickness of the mastic underneath the tile a very small amount, but if it is not extremely close to the desired thickness, you need to alter the thickness of either the plywood or the tile.

MAKING THE ISLAND BASE

1. We matched the height of our kitchen island to that of our existing kitchen counters. In our case, the counter height is 36 inches. To match your own counter, simply subtract 1½ inches from your counter height and cut the legs to that length. Cut four legs (A) from 4 x 4 pine, each measuring 34½ inches long.

2. In order to support the side rails of the kitchen island, we must remove a corner section of wood from the square top of each of the four island legs (A). Follow figure 2 to mark the area to be removed. Wrap a piece of tape around a ½-inch or ¾-inch drill bit approximately 1¾ inch from the end, or mark that place with a marking pen. Bore away as much waste as possible, stopping each hole at the depth mark on the bit. Then use a sharp chisel to cut an accurate, rectangular space, as shown in figure 2.

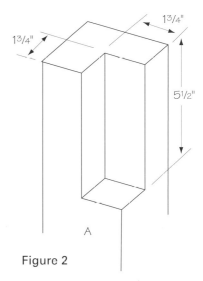

Figure 2

3. Cut two long side rails (B) from 1 x 6 pine, each measuring 38 inches long.

4. Cut two short side rails (C) from 1 x 6 pine, each measuring 20¾ inches long.

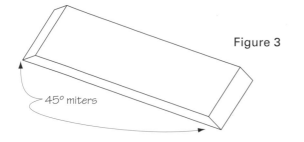

Figure 3

45° miters

5. Set each of the four side rails (B) and (C) on edge and miter both ends of each board at a 45-degree angle, as shown in figure 3.

6. This next step probably requires the assistance of a willing helper, and it should be performed on a level surface. Each of the legs (A) must be connected to the side rails (B and C) and the entire assembly must be perfectly level. It is easier to make certain that you have everything level if you perform the assembly with the legs upside down.

Carefully fit the ends of one long side rail (B) and one short side rail (C) inside the opening you cut in a leg (A), matching miters. (Refer to figure 4.) Glue and screw them in place, using two 2-inch screws through each of the side rails (B and C). Make sure that the leg is square to both adjoining side rails.

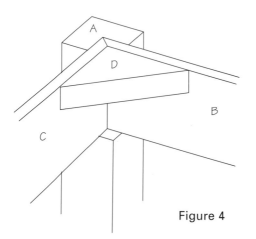

Figure 4

7. Repeat step 6 to attach the remaining three legs (A) and the remaining two side rails (B and C). A word of caution: It is easy to get involved in what you are doing and forget that you are constructing a rectangular base. The two short side rails (C) must be opposite each other on the base, and the two long side rails (B) must also be opposite each other. When all the rails are securely fastened to the legs, turn the base right side up.

8. Cut four triangular corner supports (D) from 2 x 6 pine. These should measure 5½ inches on the two short sides as shown in figure 5. Glue and screw them in each of the four corners, as shown in figure 4, flush with the top of the legs (A) and rails (B and C). Use two 3-inch screws in each corner support (D), screwing them into the side rails (B and C).

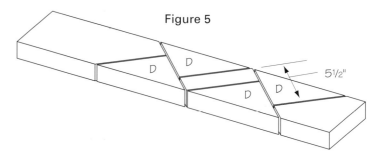

Figure 5

5½"

ADDING THE BOTTOM LAYER OF THE ISLAND TOP

9. The bottom layer of the island top adds visual thickness and also supports the center plywood. In order to avoid screw holes in the island top, the bottom layer is connected first to the island base assembly. Cut two short bottom frames (E) from 1 x 6 pine, each measuring 28¾ inches long.

10. Cut two long bottom frames (F) from 1 x 6 pine, each measuring 35 inches long.

11. Place the two short bottom frames (E) and two long bottom frames (F) on top of the base assembly. The long bottom frames (F) will fit inside the two short bottom frames (E) to form a rectangle measuring 28¾ x 46 inches, as shown in figure 6. You should have a 2¼-inch border outside each of the four legs (A). This will vary slightly if you have altered the dimensions of your island top. Clamp the bottom frames (E and F) in place.

12. Remove the bottom frames one at a time to apply glue to the top surfaces of the long and short side rails (B and C) and the corner supports (D). Screw through the bottom frames (E and F) into the side rails (B and C) using 1½-inch screws and spacing them about every 6 inches.

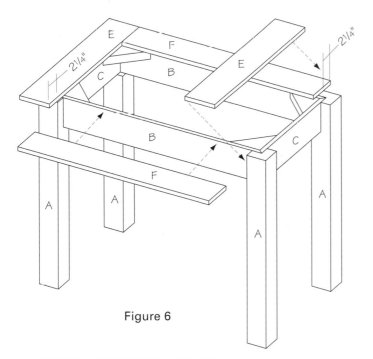

Figure 6

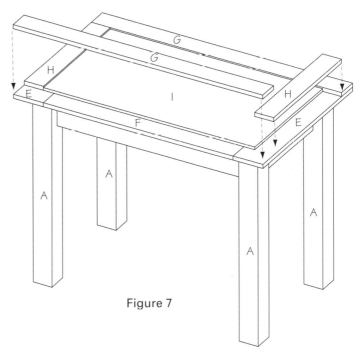

Figure 7

COMPLETING THE ISLAND TOP

13. To form the top layer, cut two long top frames (G) from 1 x 4 pine, each measuring 46 inches long.

14. Cut two short top frames (H) from 1 x 4 pine, each measuring 21¾ inches long.

15. Cut one center top (I) from ½-inch exterior plywood, measuring 21¾ x 39 inches.

16. Place the center top (I) on the base assembly and position the long and short top frames (G and H) around the center top (I), aligning the outer edges of the top frames (G and H) with the outer edges of the bottom frames (E and F) as shown in figure 7. When all five pieces are positioned correctly, carefully remove the top frames (G and H). Mark the position of the center top (I) on the bottom frames (E and F).

17. Remove the center top (I) to apply glue inside the marked area on the bottom frames (E and F). Screw through the repositioned center top (I) into the bottom frames (E and F), using 1-inch screws spaced about 6 inches apart.

18. Apply glue to the edges of the center top (I) and to the remaining top area of the bottom frames (E and F). Clamp the long and short top frames (G and H) in place and screw upward through the bottom frames (E and F) into the top frames (G and H), using 1¼-inch screws spaced about 5 inches apart in a staggered pattern.

TRIMMING THE BASE ASSEMBLY

19. The only remaining woodworking step in the island top assembly is to add the trim to the outside surfaces of the side rails (B and C). We added a length of 1 x 3 pine just under the island top and a length of 2½-inch-wide baseboard molding below that. We'll start by adding the 1 x 3 pine trim. Although our measurements should be very close to the cutting size for the trim, we suggest that you measure between your island legs before cutting each of the trim pieces, since your assembly may vary slightly. Even 1/32 inch off on the trim pieces will make your project look less than professional.

Cut two long trims (J) from 1 x 3 pine, each measuring 34½ inches long.

20. Fit the first long trim (J) between the island legs (A) against one long side rail (B). The top edge of the long trim (J) should be flush against the bottom of the island top. Apply glue to the meeting surfaces, and use 1¼-inch (3d) finish nails to attach the long trim (J) in place, spacing the nails about every 6 inches. Repeat the procedure to attach the remaining long trim (J) to the opposite side of the island.

21. Cut two short trims (K) from 1 x 3 pine, each measuring 17¼ inches in length.

22. Fit the first short trim (K) between the island legs (A) against one short side rail (C). The top edge of the short trim piece (K) should be flush against the bottom of the island top. Apply glue to the meeting surfaces, and use 1¼-inch (3d) finish nails to attach the short trim (K) in place, spacing the nails about every 6 inches. Repeat the procedure to attach the remaining short trim (K) to the opposite side of the island.

23. Cut two long moldings (L) from 2½-inch-wide baseboard molding, each measuring 34½ inches long.

24. Fit one long molding (L) beneath the long trim (J) and between the two legs (A) on one long side of the island. Apply glue to the meeting surfaces, and use 1¼-inch (3d) finish nails to attach the molding in place, spacing the nails about every 6 inches. Repeat the procedure to attach the remaining long molding (L) to the opposite side of the island.

25. Cut two short moldings (M) from 2½-inch-wide baseboard molding, each measuring 17¼ inches in length.

26. Fit the two short moldings (M) beneath the short moldings (K) on the remaining two short sides of the island, in the same manner that you used to attach the long trims (L) in step 24.

ADDING THE BOTTOM SHELF

27. Cut two long shelf supports (N) from 2 x 2 pine, each measuring 40 inches long.

28. Apply glue to the meeting surfaces, and attach one long shelf support (N) to the inside surfaces of two legs (A), 5 inches from the bottom of each leg (A), as shown in figure 8. Use two 2½-inch (8d) finish nails on each leg (A).

29. Repeat step 28 to attach the second long shelf support (N) to the inside of the remaining two legs (A).

30. Cut four short shelf supports (O) from 2 x 2 pine, each measuring 2¾ inches long.

31. Attach the four short shelf supports (O) to the remaining four inside surfaces of the four legs (A), as shown in figure 8, 5 inches from the bottom of the legs (A). Use two 2½-inch (8d) finish nails on each leg.

32. Cut one bottom shelf (P) from ¾-inch plywood, measuring 40 x 22¾ inches.

33. Following figure 9, cut a 2¾ x 2¾-inch square from each corner of the bottom shelf (P) to accommodate the legs (A).

34. Apply glue to the meeting surfaces, and fit the bottom shelf (P) over the long and short shelf supports (N and O). Nail through the bottom shelf (P) into the long and short shelf supports (N and O), using 2-inch (6d) finish nails spaced about every 3 inches.

35. Cut two long shelf trims (Q) from 1 x 4 pine, each measuring 34½ inches long.

36. Apply glue to the plywood edge, and attach one long shelf trim (Q) to one 34½-inch edge of the bottom shelf (P), flush with the upper edge. Nail through the long shelf trim (Q) into the shelf (P), using 2½-inch (8d) finish nails spaced about every 6 inches. Also nail through the long shelf trim (Q) into the ends of the short shelf supports (O).

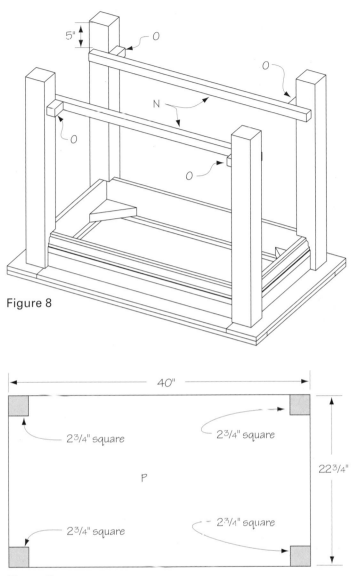

Figure 8

Figure 9

37. Repeat step 36 to attach the remaining long shelf trim (Q) to the opposite edge of the shelf (P).

38. Cut two short shelf trims (R) from 1 x 4 pine, each measuring 17¼ inches long.

39. Follow the same procedure used in step 36 to attach each of the short shelf trims (R) to the 17¼-inch edges of the shelf (P).

ADDING THE TILE

40. You may wish to mask the surface of the top frames (G and H) to protect them from stray mastic or grout. You could even apply a first coat of your finish at this point. Following the manufacturer's directions carefully, spread an even coat of tile mastic over the surface of the plywood top (I) with a trowel.

41. Place the tiles on the mastic one at a time, making sure that they are absolutely straight. Do not slide them or the mastic will be forced up on the sides of the tile. Let the mastic dry overnight.

42. Mix the tile grout according the manufacturer's directions (or use premixed grout).

43. Spread the grout over the tile using a rubber-surfaced trowel. Work in an arc and hold the trowel at an angle so that the grout is forced evenly into the spaces between the tiles.

44. When the grout begins to set up, use a damp rag to wipe the excess off of the tiles and the joints. If you let it dry, the hardened grout will be very difficult to remove. The idea is to use as little water as possible when removing the excess so that you don't thin the grout that remains. Let the grout dry overnight.

45. Rinse the remaining film from the tile and wipe it with an old towel.

46. Apply grout sealer, following the manufacturer's directions. Many grout sealers recommend that you wait several days before applying it to the project.

FINISHING

47. Fill any screw holes or imperfections in the wood with wood filler.

48. Thoroughly sand all of the wood parts on the completed island.

49. Stain or paint the wood portions of the island the color of your choice. We chose a bright white paint to match our kitchen cabinets.

DINING ROOM

Dining Table

We looked around for the perfect table for the dining room. Some were too big, some too small, and most were just too expensive. So we built this one, and we are happy with the result. It seats six comfortably, but doesn't take up the entire room.

dining table

Materials

- 32 linear feet of 1 x 4 pine
- 18 linear feet of 1 x 6 pine
- 20 linear feet of 2 x 4 pine
- Enough premade laminated pine panels to form a table top 33 x 58 inches*
- 4 newel posts, at least 27½ inches long

✱ Notes on Materials

The center of the dining table top is constructed of premade sections of laminated ¾-inch-thick pine strips, which we purchased at a building supply store. You will need enough laminated sections for a center top measuring 33 x 58 inches. Of course, you can laminate the boards yourself, but I would not suggest it unless you are an experienced woodworker and possess heavy-duty tools. If that is the case, you don't need any instructions from us on how to make it, but the trimmed size of the finished laminate should be 33 x 58 inches.

If you live in an area with distinct seasons, the cross-grain expansion and contraction that accompany alternating moist and dry conditions may cause trouble. Therefore, you should consider using a nicely veneered plywood for the center section of the table.

If you don't want to (or can't) turn table legs yourself, just purchase four newel posts from a building supply store and cut them to length. When the posts are turned upside down, who would know?

Hardware

- 36 1¼" screws
- 36 1½" screws
- 16 2½" screws
- 16 3" screws
- 28 1¼" (3d) finish nails

Special Tools and Techniques

- Long bar or pipe clamps
- Miters
- Large chisel

Cutting List

Code	Description	Qty.	Materials	Dimensions
A	Center Top	1	premade laminations	58" x 33"
B	Long Top Frame	2	1 x 4 pine	65" long
C	Short Top Frame	2	1 x 4 pine	40" long
D	Leg	4	newel posts	27½" long
E	Long Side Rail	2	2 x 4 pine	56½" long
F	Short Side Rail	2	2 x 4 pine	31½" long
G	Corner Support	4	2 x 4 pine	10" long
H	Short Bottom Frame	2	1 x 6 pine	40" long
I	Long Bottom Frame	2	1 x 6 pine	65" long
J	Long Trim	2	1 x 4 pine	53" long
K	Short Trim	2	1 x 4 pine	28" long

Constructing the Table Top

1. The initial step is to join the premade laminated sections to form a center top (A). It is a good idea to glue the sections together first and then trim the resulting laminate to the exact size. Wipe glue on the meeting edges of the laminates, and clamp them together with bar clamps for a few hours. Then trim the laminated center top (A) to 58 x 33 inches.

2. The dining table top is composed of a top and a bottom layer. The top layer consists of two long and two short frame pieces surrounding the center laminated pine. The bottom layer will be attached to the dining table base later. To form the top layer, cut two long top frames (B) from 1 x 4 pine, each measuring 65 inches long.

3. Miter the ends of each of the long frames (B) at opposing 45-degree angles, as shown in figure 1.

45° miters

Figure 1

4. Cut two short frames (C) from 1 x 4 pine, each measuring 40 inches long.

5. Miter the ends of each of the short frames (C) at opposing 45-degree angles, as shown in figure 1.

6. Place the center top (A) on a level surface. Position the short and long top frames (B and C) along the outer edges of the center top (A), as shown in figure 2. Apply glue to the meeting edges and clamp the five pieces of wood together with bar clamps for a few hours. The result is a table top that now measures 40 x 65 inches.

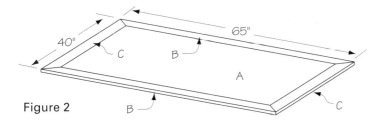

Figure 2

ADDING THE LEGS

7. Cut each of four newel posts to a length of 27½ inches to form the legs (D)

8. In order to support the side rails of the table, we must remove a corner section of wood from the square top of each of the four table legs (D). Follow figure 3 to mark the area to be removed. Use a depth stop or simply wrap a piece of tape around a ½-inch or ¾-inch drill bit approximately 1¾ inch from the end. Bore away as much waste as possible. Then use a sharp chisel to cut an accurate, 1¾ x 1¾ x 3½-inch space, as shown in figure 3.

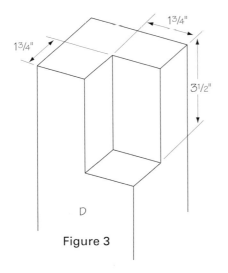

Figure 3

9. Cut two long side rails (E) from 2 x 4 pine, each measuring 56½ inches long.

10. Cut two short side rails (F) from 2 x 4 pine, each measuring 31½ inches long.

11. Set each of the four side rails (E) and (F) on edge and miter both ends of each board at a 45-degree angle, as shown in figure 4.

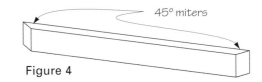

45° miters

Figure 4

12. This next step probably requires the assistance of a willing helper, and it should be performed on a level surface. Each of the legs (D) must be connected to the side rails (E and F), and the entire assembly must be perfectly level. It is easier to make certain that you have everything level if you perform the assembly with the legs upside down.

Carefully fit the ends of one long rail (E) and one short rail (F) inside the opening that you previously cut in the leg (D), matching miters (refer to figure 5.) Glue and screw them in place, using two 2½-inch screws through each end of the side rails (E and F).

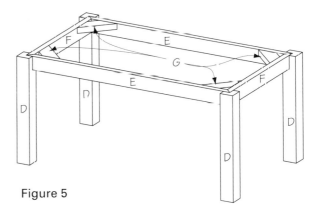

Figure 5

13. Repeat step 12 to attach the remaining three legs (D) to the remaining two side rails (E and F). A word of caution: It is easy to get involved in what you are doing and forget that you are constructing a rectangular base. The two short side rails (F) must be opposite each other on the base and the two long side rails (E) must also be opposite each other.

14. Cut four corner supports (G) from 2 x 4 pine, each measuring 10 inches long.

15. Miter both ends of each of the four corner supports (G) at opposing 45-degree angles, as shown in figure 1.

16. Glue and screw the corner supports (G) in each of the four corners, as shown in figure 5, flush with the tops of the legs (D) and the long and short rails (E and F). Use two 3-inch screws in each corner support (G), driving them into the side rails (E and F).

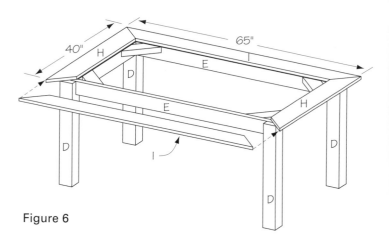

Figure 6

ADDING THE TABLE TOP BOTTOM LAYER

17. The bottom layer of the table top adds visual thickness and also supports the laminated center top (A). In order to avoid screw holes in the table top, the bottom layer is connected first to the table base assembly. The bottom layer consists of four additional lengths of wood cut from 1 x 6 pine. Cut two short bottom frames (H) from 1 x 6 pine, each measuring 40 inches long.

18. Miter both ends of each of the two short bottom frames (H) at opposing 45-degree angles, as shown in figure 1.

19. Cut two long bottom frames (I) from 1 x 6 pine, each measuring 65 inches long.

20. Miter both ends of each of the two long bottom frames (I) at opposing 45-degree angles, as shown in figure 1.

21. Place the four bottom frames (H and I) on the base assembly and fit them together to form a rectangle, measuring 65 x 40, as shown in figure 6. This rectangle will extend past the legs (D) by 2½ inches on each side. When you are satisfied with the arrangement, glue and screw the bottom frames (H and I) to the long and short side rails (E and F) and to the corner supports (G), using 1½-inch screws spaced about 6 inches apart. Use two 3-inch screws to screw through the bottom frame pieces (H and I) into each of the table legs (D).

JOINING THE TABLE TOP TO THE BASE

22. Turn the top assembly (pieces A, B, and C) upside down on a flat surface. Make certain that the best side of the laminate is on the bottom. Place the base assembly upside down over the top assembly. The two short bottom frame pieces (H) and the two long bottom frame pieces (I) should be flush with the outer edges of the top assembly, as shown in figure 7. The inside edges of the bottom frame pieces (H and I) will overlap the center top (A) by 2 inches. Apply glue to the meeting faces of all four bottom frame pieces (H and I), and screw through pieces H and I into pieces A, B, and C. Use four 1¼-inch screws on each of the short bottom frames (H), and five 1¼-inch screws on each of the long bottom frames (I), spacing them evenly along the outside edges of the boards. Use the same numbers of screws spaced along the inside edges of the bottom frames (H and I), attaching them securely to the center top (A). Allow the glue to dry.

23. The remaining step in the table assembly is to add the trim to the outside surfaces of the side rails (E and F). We added a length of 1 x 4 pine over the 2 x 4 rails just under the table top. Although our measurements should be very close to the cutting size for the trim, we suggest that you measure between your table legs before cutting each of the trim pieces, since your assembly may vary slightly. Even ¹⁄₃₂ inch off on the trim pieces will make your project look less than professional. Cut two long trims (J) from 1 x 4 pine, each measuring 53 inches long.

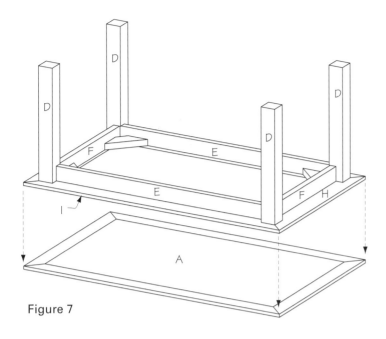

Figure 7

29. Fill the screw holes, crevices, and cracks with wood filler.

30. Sand all surfaces of the completed table.

31. Stain or paint the table the color of your choice. We chose to retain the natural color of the pine in the center of the table and to paint the rest of the table a bright white. We then sealed it with several coats of high gloss polyurethane.

24. Fit the first long trim (J) between the table legs (D) on one long side of the table against the one long side rail (E). The top edge of the long trim (J) should be flush against the bottom of the table top. Apply glue to the meeting surfaces, and use 1¼-inch (3d) finish nails to attach the long trim (J) in place, spacing the nails about every 6 inches.

25. Repeat the procedure to attach the remaining long trim (J) to the opposite side of the table.

26. Cut two short trims (K) from 1 x 4 pine, each measuring 28 inches long.

27. Fit the first short trim (K) between the table legs (D) on one short side of the table against one short side rail (F). The top edge of the short trim piece (K) should be flush against the bottom of the table top. Apply glue to the meeting surfaces and use 1¼-inch (3d) finish nails to attach the short trim (K) in place, spacing the nails about every 6 inches.

28. Repeat step 27 to attach the remaining short trim (K) to the opposite side of the table.

Buffet

If you need a stylish buffet for your dining room, this is it! Not only is it inexpensive to build, but its expensive-looking finish is easier to accomplish than sanding and painting. And its square drawers are prefect for storing napkins, napkin rings, and other dining necessities.

Materials

- 4 linear feet of 1 x 1 pine
- 6 linear feet of 1 x 2 pine
- 50 linear feet of 1 x 4 pine
- 16 linear feet of 1 x 6 pine
- 6 linear feet of 2 x 4 pine
- 14" x 24" piece of ¼" plywood
- 1 sheet (4' x 8') of ¾" plywood
- 6 linear feet of 4" PVC pipe

Hardware

- 48 2" (6d) finish nails
- 28 1¼" wood screws
- 210 1½" wood screws
- 12 2" wood screws
- 36 3" wood screws
- Four drawer pulls

Special Tools and Techniques

- Heavy-duty double-sided tape
- Hand plane
- Router with ⅜" round-over cutter (optional)
- Dadoes

Cutting List

Code	Description	Qty.	Materials	Dimensions
A	Top/Bottom	2	¾" plywood	12½" x 48"
B	Side	2	¾" plywood	9½" x 12½"
C	Vertical Trim	5	1 x 4 pine	11" long
D	Horizontal Trim	8	1 x 2 pine	7⅝" long
E	Trim Support	1	1 x 1 pine	46½" long
F	Base Top/Bottom	2	¾" plywood	12½" x 48"
G	Large Leg Support	4	2 x 4 pine	17½" long
H	Small Leg Support	4	1 x 4 pine	17½" long
I	Base Side	2	1 x 4 pine	12½" long
J	Base Front/Back	2	1 x 4 pine	48" long
K	Small Leg	4	1 x 4 pine	3½" long
L	Large Leg	4	1 x 6 pine	5½" long
M	Outer Leg	4	4" PVC pipe	17½" long
N	Long Bottom Support	2	1 x 4 pine, ripped	46½" long
O	Short Bottom Support	2	1 x 4 pine ripped	11" long
P	Long Guide	8	1 x 4 pin	12½" long
Q	Short Guide	8	1 x 4 pine	11" long
R	Back	1	¾" plywood	11" x 48"
S	Drawer Front/Back	8	1 x 6 pine	7½" long
T	Drawer Side	8	1 x 6 pine	10½" long
U	Drawer Bottom	4	¼" plywood	6⅜" x 10⅜"
V	Drawer Front	4	½" plywood	9¾" square

MAKING THE TOP SECTION

1. Cut two top/bottoms (A) from ¾-inch plywood, each measuring 48 x 12½ inches.

2. Cut two sides (B) from ¾-inch plywood, each measuring 9½ x 12½ inches.

3. Place the two top/bottoms (A) on a level surface, parallel to each other and 9½ inches apart. Fit the two sides (B) between the ends of the two top/bottoms (A), as shown in figure 1. Apply glue to the meeting surfaces, and screw through the top/bottoms (A) into the edges of the sides (B), using four 1½-inch screws on each joint.

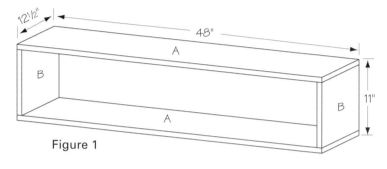

Figure 1

4. Cut five vertical trims (C) from 1 x 4 pine, each measuring 11 inches long.

5. Refer to figure 2 to attach each of the five vertical trims (C) across the open front of the buffet top. The first vertical trim (C) should be flush with the outer edges of the sides (B) and exactly cover the edges of both top/bottoms (A). Screw through the vertical trim (C) into the edges of the top/bottoms (A), using two 1½-inch screws, and into the edges of the sides (B), using two 1½-inch screws.

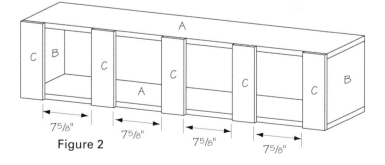

Figure 2

6. Repeat step 5 to attach a second vertical trim (C) to the opposite side of the assembly.

7. The third vertical trim (C) should be positioned 7⅝ inches from the first. Screw through the ends of the vertical trim (C) into both of the top/bottoms (A), using three 1½-inch screws on each joint.

8. Repeat step 7 to attach the fourth vertical trim (C) 7⅝ inches from the third.

9. Repeat step 7 to attach the fifth vertical trim (C) 7⅝ inches from the fourth and second.

10. Cut eight horizontal trims (D) from 1 x 2 pine, each measuring 7⅝ inches long.

11. Apply glue to the meeting surfaces, and screw one horizontal trim (D) to the top/bottom (A) between each pair of vertical trims (C) as shown in figure 3. Use three 1½-inch screws on each vertical trim (C).

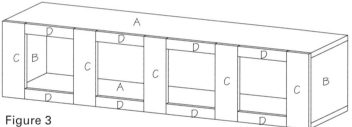

Figure 3

12. To reinforce the joints between the horizontal and vertical trims (C and D), cut one trim support (E) from 1 x 1 pine measuring 46½ inches long. You can rip this piece from one of the pieces of 1 x 4 pine to be used for the long bottom supports (N).

13. Apply glue to the meeting surfaces, and screw the trim support (E) to the inside of the cabinet, against the horizontal and vertical trims (C and D) and the top (A). Note that there is only one trim support and that it will be at the top of the finished buffet. The lower horizontal and vertical trims (C and D) will be reinforced later. Screw through the trim supports (C and D) and the top (A) using 1¼-inch screws spaced about every 6 inches.

MAKING THE BASE

14. Cut two base top/bottoms (F) from ¾-inch plywood, each measuring 12½ x 46½ inches long.

15. The four round legs that connect the base to the top of the buffet are lengths of PVC pipe which are reinforced by wooden supports. Cut four large leg supports (G) from 2 x 4 pine, each measuring 17½ inches long.

16. Cut four small leg supports (H) from 1 x 4 pine, each measuring 17½ inches long.

17. Glue each large leg support (G) to one small leg support (H), matching ends and edges, to make a leg support assembly 2¼ inches thick. Either clamp the pieces together for an hour or drive three 1½-inch screws through each small leg support (H) into its large leg support (G).

18. Try to slide each leg support assembly (G/H) into a length of 4-inch PVC pipe. Using a hand plane, chamfer the corners of the leg support assemblies (G/H) until each slides easily into the pipe.

19. Following the measurements in figure 4, draw four 2¼ x 3½-inch rectangles on one of the base top/bottoms (F). This will be the exact placement for the four leg support assemblies (G/H).

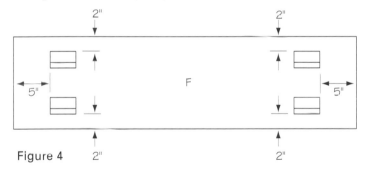

Figure 4

20. Attach the four leg support assemblies (G/H) to the base top (F), placing them exactly over the rectangles that you drew. Screw through the base top (F) into the leg support assemblies (G/H), using four 3-inch screws on each leg support assembly (G/H).

21. Cut two base sides (I) from 1 x 4 pine, each measuring 12½ inches long.

22. Place the two base top/bottoms (F) on their long edges on a level surface, parallel to each other and 2 inches apart. Use props under two of the leg support assemblies (G/H). Place one base side (I) over the 12½-inch edges of both base top/bottoms (F), as shown in figure 5. Apply glue to the meeting surfaces, and screw through the base side (I) into the ends of both of the base top/bottoms, using four 1½-inch screws on each joint.

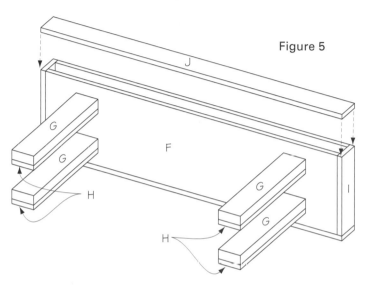

Figure 5

23. Repeat step 4 to attach the remaining base side (I) to the opposite ends of the two base top/bottoms (F).

24. Cut two base front/backs (J) from 1 x 4 pine, each measuring 48 inches long.

25. Place one base front/back (J) over the base assembly, flush with the outer surfaces of the two base top/bottoms (F) and the two base sides (I), as shown in figure 5. Apply glue to the meeting surfaces, and screw through the base front/back (J) into the edges of the two base top/bottoms (F) and the two base sides (I), using 1½-inch screws spaced 6 inches apart.

26. Turn the base assembly over and repeat step 25 to fasten the remaining base front/back (J) to the other side of the base assembly.

27. Cut four small legs (K) from 1 x 4 pine, each measuring 3½ inches long.

28. Cut four large legs (L) from 1 x 6 pine, each measuring 5½ inches long.

29. Center one small leg (K) over one large leg (L), as shown in figure 6. Apply glue to the back of the small leg (K), reposition it on the large leg (L), and screw through the small leg (K) into the large leg (L). Use three 1¼-inch screws on each joint.

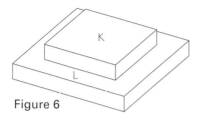

Figure 6

30. Repeat step 29 three more times using the remaining three small legs (K) and three large legs (L).

31. Apply glue to the top of one small leg (K), and attach one leg assembly (K/L) to one corner of the base assembly. The large leg (L) portion of the leg assembly should be even with the outer edges of the base assembly. Screw through the leg assembly into the base assembly, using three 2-inch screws.

32. Repeat step 31 three more times to attach the remaining three leg assemblies to the remaining three corners of the base assembly.

CONNECTING THE BASE AND TOP ASSEMBLIES

33. Cut four outer legs (M) from 4-inch PVC pipe, each measuring 17½ inches long.

34. Place the base assembly right side up and slide the four outer legs (M) over the leg support assemblies (G/H). Center the top assembly over the legs, making certain that the sides and front of the top assembly are exactly even with the sides and front of the base assembly. Use a straightedge held against those surfaces to check the accuracy of your alignment. Also make certain that the trim support (E) is on the inside upper edge of the top assembly. Then screw through the inside of the top assembly into each of the four leg support assemblies (G/H), using four 3-inch screws on each joint.

MAKING THE DRAWER GUIDES

35. Rip a total of 11 feet of 1 x 4 pine to 2½ inches in width.

36. Cut two long bottom supports (N) from the ripped material, each measuring 46½ inches long.

37. Cut two short bottom supports (O) from the ripped material, each measuring 11 inches long.

38. Place the two long bottom supports (N) on a level surface, parallel to each other, on edge, and 11 inches apart. Place the two short bottom supports (O), between the two long bottom supports (N), as shown in figure 7. Screw through the long bottom supports (N) into the short bottom supports (O) using two 1½-inch screws on each joint.

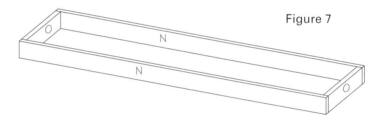

Figure 7

39. Cut eight long guides (P) from 1 x 4 pine, each measuring 12½ inches long.

40. Cut eight short guides (Q) from 1 x 4 pine, each measuring 11 inches long.

41. Screw and glue one short guide (Q) to one long guide (P), as shown in figure 8, leaving a ¾-inch space at each end of the long guide (P). Note that the back face of the long guide (P) should be flush with the back edge of the short guide (Q). Fasten the pieces with glue and three 1½-inch screws, spacing them evenly along the joint.

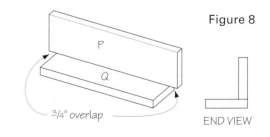

Figure 8

3/4" overlap

END VIEW

42. Repeat step 40 seven more times, using the remaining seven long guides (P) and seven short guides (Q).

43. Attach the guide assemblies to the support assembly, as shown in figure 9. Position all the pieces and mark their locations. Then slide the marked support assembly into the top assembly to check the locations of the long guides (P). The long guides (P) will butt against the backs of the vertical trims (C), with the face of each long guide (P) flush with an edge of its vertical trim (C). Begin on the left side, placing the first guide assembly with its short guide (Q) portion inside the support assembly and with the outer face of its long guide portion (P) 1¼ inches from the end of the support assembly.

44. Position the second guide assembly so that the long guide (H) portion is 7⅝ inches from that of the first guide assembly.

45. Position the third assembly so that the long guide (H) portions of the second and third assemblies are 2 inches apart.

46. Repeat steps 43 and 44 to add the remaining guide assemblies, as shown in figure 9.

47. When you are sure that the spacing is exactly correct, secure each of the guide assemblies to the support assembly. Screw through each of the long supports (N) into the ends of the short guide (Q) portions of the guide assemblies. Use two 1½-inch screws on each of the joints.

48. Slide the entire guide/support assembly inside the back of the top assembly. Check the alignment, and then screw through the front vertical trims (C) into the ends of each of the guide assemblies. Use two 1½-inch screws on each of the joints.

49. Cut one back (R) from ¾-inch plywood, measuring 11 x 48 inches.

50. Fit the back (R) over the edges of the top/bottoms (A) and the sides (B). Apply glue to the meeting surfaces, and screw through the back (R) into the edges of the top/bottoms (A) and sides (B), using 1½-inch screws spaced about every 6 inches.

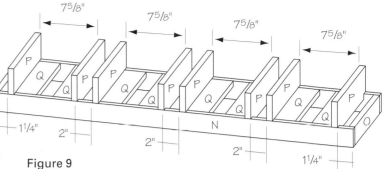

Figure 9

MAKING THE DRAWERS

There are four identical drawers in this buffet. All four are constructed as shown in the assembly diagram in figure 10.

51. Cut eight drawer front/backs (S) from 1 x 6 pine, each measuring 7½ inches long.

52. Cut eight drawer sides (T) from 1 x 6 pine, each measuring 10½ inches long.

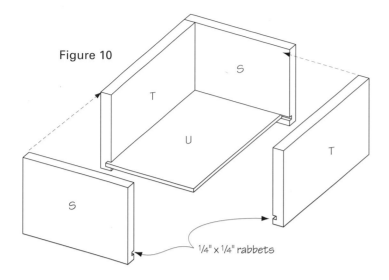

Figure 10

1/4" x 1/4" rabbets

53. Cut a ¼ x ¼-inch dado on the inside of each drawer piece (S and T), ⅜ inch from the lower edge, to accommodate the plywood bottom.

54. Cut four drawer bottoms (U) from ¼-inch plywood, measuring 6⅜ x 10⅜ inches.

55. Assemble one drawer as shown in figure 10. Note that the drawer front/back pieces (S) overlap the ends of the drawer sides (T). Use three 2-inch (6d) finish nails on each end of the overlapping boards. The drawer front (V) will be added later.

56. Repeat the drawer assembly three times using the remaining six drawer front/backs (S), the six drawer sides (T), and the three drawer bottoms (U).

ADDING THE DRAWER FRONTS

57. Cut four drawer fronts (U) from ½-inch plywood, each measuring 9¾ inches square.

58. Drill a 3/16-inch hole through the exact center of each drawer front (V) to act as a guide for installing the drawer pulls later.

59. For a more finished appearance, round the edges of the front side of the drawer fronts (V) using a hand plane or a router.

60. To attach the drawer fronts (V) to the assembled drawers, set each of the drawers inside the drawer openings, on top of the drawer glides. Place a piece of wood between the back of each drawer and the back of the buffet so that the drawers are held just proud of the front of the buffet. Use heavy-duty double-sided tape to hold a drawer front temporarily in place on each drawer until you have all four drawer fronts positioned exactly right. The drawer fronts should be level with each other, centered vertically on the front of the top assembly, and the spacing should be equal on both sides of the center drawers. Then attach the fronts to the drawers. Use three 1-inch screws, countersunk ⅛ inch, to screw through the drawer into the drawer front (V).

FINISHING

61. We used a ⅜-inch round-over cutter in a router to round all the edges of the top and bottom assembly. This treatment complements the textured finish, but it is not necessary if you plan to simply paint your buffet.

62. We finished our buffet by marbleizing the legs and covering the top, base, and feet with textured sand finish. If you plan to do the same, you need sand only the PVC pipe so that it will accept a coat of paint. Because the textured sand finish is so thick, it is not necessary to fill or sand the wood prior to texturing. And because the textured finish is off-white, we did not paint the textured areas (although you certainly can, if you prefer a different color).

We also used a marbleizing kit to paint the legs. Simply follow the manufacturer's directions to achieve the same result.

If you plan to paint or stain your buffet, you first must fill any screw holes, cracks, and crevices with wood filler and thoroughly sand the entire project.

63. Install the drawer pulls, centering them on each of the four drawers, and screwing through the inside of the drawer into the drawer pulls, using a 3-inch screw.

Mirror

Want a great re-do for an old mirror? Frame it with ready-made trim and decorative squares. It's easy and inexpensive. And the frame can be adjusted to fit any size mirror. We spray-painted our mirror frame a bronze color to match our buffet.

Materials

- 12 linear feet of 1 x 4 pine
- 12 linear feet of 3" beaded molding
- 4 decorative squares, each measuring 4" square
- 1 mirror, 26⅜" x 40⅜" x ¼" thick

Hardware

- 8 corrugated metal fasteners
- 30 ¾" brads
- 12 1¼" (3d) finish nails
- 2 screw eyes, ⅜" diameter
- Picture-hanging wire

Special Tools and Techniques

- Chisel
- Router with rabbet cutter
- Rabbets

Cutting List

Code	Description	Qty	Materials	Dimensions
A	Top/Bottom	2	1 x 4 pine	46" long
B	Side	2	1 x 4 pine	25" long
C	Decorative Square	4	purchased	4" x 4"
D	Long Beaded Molding	2	3" wide	cut to fit (39" long)
E	Short Beaded Molding	2	3" wide	cut to fit (25" long)

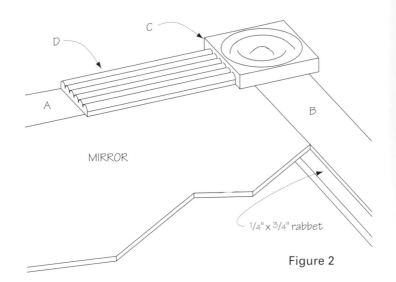

MIRROR

1/4" x 3/4" rabbet

Figure 2

BUILDING THE FRAME

1. Cut two top/bottoms (A) from 1 x 4 pine, each measuring 46 inches long.

2. Cut two sides (B) from 1 x 4 pine, each measuring 25 inches long.

3. Place the two top/bottoms (A) on a level surface, parallel to each other and 25 inches apart. Fit the two sides (B) between the two top/bottoms (A) to form a 32 x 46-inch rectangle, as shown in figure 1. Use two corrugated fasteners on each joint to hold the four pieces together. Place the inner fastener at least 1 inch from the inside of the frame.

4. Rout the inside edges of the assembled rectangle, 1/4-inch deep and 3/4-inch wide. Use a chisel to cut the corners of this rabbet square.

5. Place the mirror into the rabbet in the rectangular frame. The front surface of the mirror should be flush with the front of the rectangular frame.

ADDING THE TRIM

6. Refer to the project photograph and to figure 2 to place the trim on the mirror. Begin by placing the four decorative squares (C) at the four corners of the rectangular frame. They should extend over the outside of the rectangular frame by 1/2 inch on each side. Use spring clamps or weights to hold the decorative squares (C) in place while you fit the long and short beaded moldings (D and E).

7. The beaded moldings (D and E) lie flush with the outside edge of the rectangular frame and fit between the decorative squares (C). Furthermore, the 3-inch-wide beaded moldings (D and E) must be centered widthwise on the 4-inch decorative squares (C). Measuring between the clamped decorative squares (C), cut the long beaded moldings (D) and the short beaded moldings (E) to fit. Lay the beaded moldings (D and E) in place and make sure that all the joints are snug.

8. Apply glue to the rectangular frame under each beaded molding (D or E), and nail through the beaded molding, using 3/4-inch brads spaced every 4 inches.

9. Remove the clamps or weights from the decorative squares (C). Glue and nail the four decorative squares (C) in place, using three 1 1/4-inch (3d) finish nails through each of the decorative squares (C).

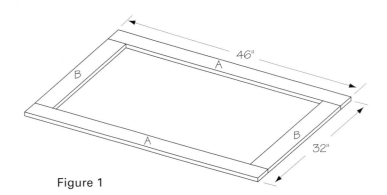

46"

32"

Figure 1

FINISHING

10. Fill any screw holes or imperfections in the wood with wood filler.

11. Thoroughly sand all surfaces of the completed mirror.

12. Stain or paint the mirror the color of your choice. We chose a bronze paint to coordinate with our buffet.

13. Install one ⅜ inch screw eye in the back of each side (B) approximately 8 inches from the top of the completed frame. Connect the screw eyes with heavy-duty picture-hanging wire, following the manufacturer's recommendations.

repetition, repetition!

Professional interior designers unify a room—or a whole house—by repeating key design elements. You might play with color first. In our house, which you see photographed in this book, we painted most of the walls white. Using the same wall color allows the eye to flow from one room to another, whereas different colored walls break the flow. Repetition unifies!

Repeated or complementary design elements define a style in furniture as well. In this photograph, which straddles our dining and living rooms, the mirror frame and the corner cabinet are trimmed with the same molding and decorative squares. We painted both pieces with a bronze finish (repeated in the drawer pulls on the buffet) and, to carry the eye from one to the other, we aligned the top of the mirror with the top of the corner cabinet.

Tiled Coffee Table

This coffee table is probably the most rugged one ever. Its tile top is almost indestructible and will withstand spilled drinks, kids' toys, and just about anything else. And putting it together is lots of fun, too. Fitting the broken tile pieces together is like completing a giant jigsaw puzzle—even the kids helped!

Materials

- 50 linear feet of 1 x 4 pine
- 1 linear foot of 2 x 6 pine
- 1 piece of ½" plywood, 46 x 46 inches
- 15 linear feet of ¾"-wide decorative molding
- 4 newel posts with 3½" x 3½" square end*
- Enough ceramic tiles to cover a 46" x 46" area*
- Tile grout (small container)
- Tile mastic (small container)
- Grout sealer (small bottle)

*Notes on Materials

If you don't own a lathe or don't want to turn the table legs yourself, just purchase four newel posts from a building supply store and cut them to length. Turned upside down, they make extremely good-looking table legs!

When choosing the tile for this table, consider that the tile must fit in a specified area. We covered the center of the table with broken tile. If you would rather have whole tile covering the top of the coffee table, you will have some additional figuring to do. If the tile you like will not fit evenly into the dimensions of the plywood center, you can either alter the dimensions of the table or trim some of the tiles. We suggest that you read through the section "Constructing the Table Top," which explains how to make certain that your tiles fit the project. If you opt to trim the tile to fit the table dimensions, you will need a tile cutter.

To install the tiles, you need a trowel for spreading the mastic and a rubber-surfaced trowel for applying the grout.

Hardware

- 64 1" screws
- 32 1¼" screws
- 32 1½" screws
- 16 2" screws
- 8   2½" screws
- 8   3" screws

Special Tools and Techniques:

- 3 or 4 large bar or pipe clamps
- Large chisel
- Trowel
- Rubber-surfaced trowel
- Tile cutter (if necessary)*
- Miters

Cutting List

Code	Description	Qty	Materials	Dimensions
A	Leg	4	newel post	14½" long
B	Side Rail	4	1 x 4 pine	45½" long
C	Triangular Support	4	2 x 6 pine	5½" on short sides
D	Top Trim	4	1 x 4 pine	50" long
E	Center	1	½" plywood	46" x 46"
F	Top Frame	4	1 x 4 pine, ripped	50" long
G	SideTrim	4	decorative molding	42" long

MAKING THE TABLE BASE

1. To form the legs (A), cut each of the four newel posts to a length of 14½ inches.

2. In order to support the side rails of the coffee table, we must remove a corner section of wood from the square top of each of the four legs (A). Follow figure 1 to mark the area to be removed. Use a depth stop or simply wrap a piece of tape around a ½-inch or ¾-inch drill bit approximately 1¾-inch from the end. Bore away as much waste as possible. Then use a sharp chisel to cut an accurate, rectangular space, as shown in figure 1.

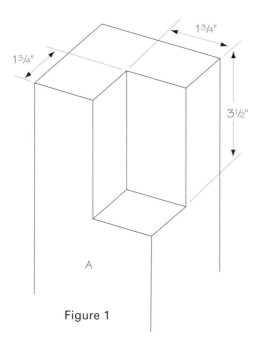

Figure 1

3. Cut four side rails (B) from 1 x 4 pine, each measuring 45½ inches long. Miter both ends of each side rail (B) at opposing 45-degree angles, as shown in figure 2.

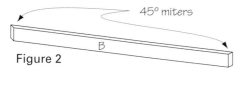

Figure 2

4. The next assembly will probably require the assistance of a willing helper and must be performed on a level surface. Each of the legs (A) must be connected to the side rails (B), and the entire assembly must be perfectly level. It is easier to make certain that everything is level if you perform the assembly with the legs upside down. Carefully fit two of the side rails (B), matching miters, inside the opening that you cut in one of the legs (A), as shown (right side up) in figure 3. Apply glue to the meeting surfaces, and screw through the side rails (B) into the legs (A), using two 2-inch screws on each of the joints. Make sure that the leg (A) is square to both of the adjoining side rails (B).

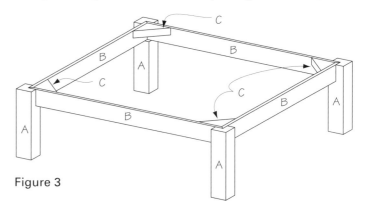

Figure 3

5. Repeat step 4 three more times to attach the remaining three legs (A) to the remaining side rails (B), as shown in figure 3.

6. Cut four triangular supports (C) from 2 x 6 pine, measuring 5½ inches on the two short sides, as shown in figure 4. Apply glue to the mitered surfaces, and screw through the triangular supports (C) into the side rails (B) in the four corners of the table base, as shown in figure 3. The triangular supports (C) should be flush with the tops of the side rails (B). Use two 3-inch screws on each support.

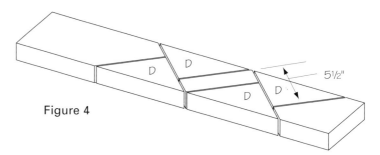

Figure 4

CONSTRUCTING THE TABLE TOP

The table top consists of a center piece of ½-inch-thick plywood that is framed on all four sides with lengths of 2-inch-wide pine. The difference in thickness between the ½-inch-thick plywood and the ¾-inch-thick pine allows for the addition of ceramic tile in the center of the table.

We circumvented the need to figure exact area for tile placement on our coffee table by simply using odd-sized broken tiles. In order to ensure a flat table top when you are finished, you must check that the thickness of the plywood plus the thickness of the tile (and any tile mastic that you place under the tile) is equal to the thickness of the 1 x 4 pine that borders the table. You can vary the thickness of the mastic underneath the tile a very small amount, but if it is not extremely close to the desired thickness, you need to alter the thickness of either the plywood or the tile.

If you decide to use whole tiles, then you will need to do some additional figuring to make certain that the tiles you have bought will fit the dimensions we have given. In the event that they do not, you will need to alter the dimensions of the table top pieces to accommodate your own tiles. To verify your own dimensions, arrange your tiles on your uncut piece of ½-inch-thick plywood. Measure the area your tiles cover, allowing for a border of grout around the outer edges the same width as the grout between the tiles.

Draw a line around the tiles (including the outer grout allowance), forming a square. Compare the dimensions of your square to the size specified in the instructions for the center (E). If it deviates from those measurements (46 inches square), you must adjust the size of the center plywood, and also the lengths of all of the additional table top pieces (D, E, and F).

Actually, if the new size differs by more than ½ inch, the side rails should be adjusted, too. Here is a formula for changing all the other dimentions: if your dimensions are over 46 inches square, you must add the difference to all of the pieces except the legs (A). If your dimensions are under 46 inches square, you must subtract the difference from all the pieces except the legs (A).

7. The table top is composed of a top and bottom layer. The top layer consists of four frame pieces surrounding the center plywood. The bottom layer is made of wider frame pieces which support both the center plywood and the top frame. To form the bottom layer, cut four top trims (D) from 1 x 4 pine, each measuring 50 inches long.

8. Miter both ends of each top trim (D) at opposing 45-degree angles, as shown in figure 5.

Figure 5

9. The top trims (D) lay flat on top of the base assembly. Their miters should align with the miters of the side rails (B), they should extend inward past the sides rails (B) by ½ inch, and they should extend outward past the legs (A) by ½ inch, as shown in figure 6. Apply glue to the top edge of each side rail (B), and screw through each top trim (D) into a side rail (B). Use 1½-inch screws spaced about every 6 inches. Use a 2½-inch screw to fasten each end of each top trim (D) to the top of its leg (A), making sure that the top faces of the top trims (D) are flush.

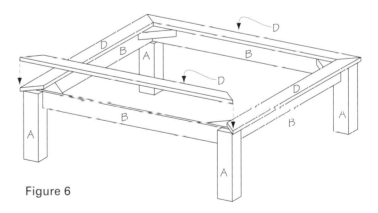

Figure 6

10. Cut one center (E) from ½-inch-thick plywood, 46 x 46 inches square.

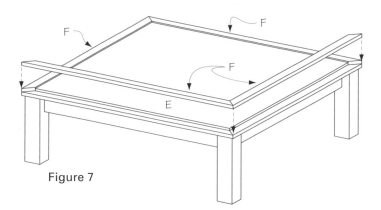

Figure 7

11. Apply glue to the meeting surfaces, and position the center (E) over the top trims (D), matching the corners of the center (E) to the mitered joints between the top trims (D), as shown in figure 7. Screw through the center (E) into the top trims (D), using 1-inch screws spaced every 6 inches or so.

12. Cut four top frames (F) from 1 x 4 pine, each measuring slightly over 50 inches long. Rip each top frame (F) to 2 inches in width.

13. Miter the ends of each top frame (F) at opposing 45-degree angles, as shown in figure 5, so that the shorter mitered edge matches an edge of the center (E).

14. Apply glue to the edges of the center (E), the top surfaces of the top trims (D), and the mitered surfaces of the top frames (F). Clamp the top frames (F) to the top trims (D) as shown in figure 7. The outside of the top frames (F) should be flush with the edges of the top trims (D). Screw from the bottom through the top trims (D) into the top frames (F), using 1¼-inch screws placed 1 inch from the outside of the top trims (D) and spaced about 6 inches apart.

ADDING THE SIDE TRIMS

15. Cut four side trims (G) from ¾-inch-wide decorative molding, each measuring 42 inches long.

16. Apply glue to the back of the side trims (G) and glue and nail them centered on the outside of the side rails (B). To avoid holes in the molding, clamp the two pieces together and screw through the side rails (B) into the side trim pieces (G). Use 1-inch-long screws, spacing them about every 5 inches.

ADDING THE TILE

17. You may wish to mask the surfaces of the top frames (F) to protect them from stray mastic or grout. You could even apply a first coat of your finish at this point. Following the manufacturer's directions carefully, spread an even coat of tile mastic over the surface of the plywood center (E) with a trowel.

18. Place the tile pieces on the mastic one at a time. Do not slide them or the mastic will be forced up on the sides of the tile. Let the mastic dry overnight.

19. Mix the tile grout according the manufacturer's directions (or use premixed grout).

20. Spread the grout over the tile using a rubber-surfaced trowel. Work in an arc, and hold the trowel at an angle so that the grout is forced evenly into the spaces between the tiles.

21. When the grout begins to set up, use a damp rag to wipe the excess off the tiles and the joints. If you let it dry, the hardened grout will be very difficult to remove. The idea is to use as little water as possible when removing the excess so that you don't thin the grout that remains. Let the grout dry overnight.

22. Rinse the remaining film from the tile and wipe it with an old towel.

23. Apply grout sealer, following the manufacturer's directions. Many grout sealers recommend that you wait several days before applying it to the project.

FINISHING

24. Fill any screw holes or imperfections in the wood with wood filler.

25. Thoroughly sand all of the wood parts on the completed coffee table.

26. Stain or paint the wood portions of the coffee table the color of your choice. We chose an off-white paint.

Corner Cupboard

Here's a great way to perk up a lost corner. Build this corner cabinet and fill it with all your favorite things! The shelves are tall enough to accommodate pictures, your tallest knickknacks, and a huge vase of flowers.

corner cupboard

Materials

- 3 linear feet of 1 x 6 pine
- 18 linear feet of 2 x 2 pine
- 18 linear feet of 3-inch-wide beaded molding
- 1½ sheets (4' x 8') of ¾" plywood
- 4 decorative pine squares

Hardware

- 42 1⅝" wood screws
- 82 1¼" (3d) finish nails
- 12 1¼" (4d) finish nails

Special Tools and Techniques

- Bevels
- Miters

Cutting List

Code	Description	Qty.	Materials	Dimensions
A	Wide Side	1	¾" plywood	23" x 72"
B	Narrow Side	1	¾" plywood	22¼" x 72"
C	Top	1	¾" plywood	21½" x 21½" x 30½" triangular
D	Shelf	1	¾" plywood	21½" x 21½" x 30½" triangular
E	Bottom	1	¾" plywood	21½" x 21½" x 30½" triangular
F	Bottom Trim	1	1 x 6 pine	34½" long
G	Support Strips	2	2 x 2 pine	cut to fit
H	Beveled Strips	4	2 x 2 pine	cut to fit
I	Decorative Squares	4	premade	4 x 4 inches
J	Beaded Trim	6	3"-wide beaded trim	cut to fit

MAKING THE CUPBOARD

1. Cut one wide side (A) from ¾-inch plywood, measuring 23 x 72 inches.

2. Bevel one 72-inch edge at a 45-degree angle, as shown in figure 1.

3. Cut one narrow side (B) from 3/4-inch plywood, measuring 22¼ x 72 inches.

4. Bevel one 72-inch edge at a 45-degree angle, as shown in figure 1.

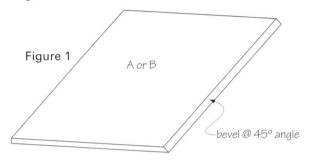

Figure 1

A or B

bevel @ 45° angle

5. Place the narrow side (B) flat on a level surface, with the beveled edge facing upward. Place the unbeveled 72-inch edge of the wide side (A) against the 72-inch unbeveled edge of the narrow side, as shown in figure 2. When the pieces are correctly positioned, you should be able to place a straightedge flat against both beveled edges (as shown in figure 2). Apply glue to the meeting surfaces, and screw through the wide side (A) into the edge of the narrow side (B). Use 1⅝-inch screws spaced about every 6 inches.

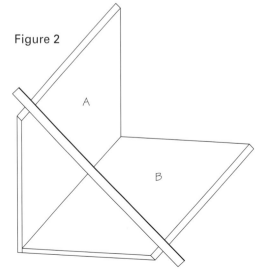

Figure 2

A

B

6. Cut three right triangles from ¾-inch plywood, each measuring 21½ inches on the short sides. Label one piece top (C), one shelf (D), and one bottom (E).

7. Attach the top (C) flush with the top edges of the wide and narrow sides (A and B), as shown in figure 3. Apply glue to the meeting surfaces, and screw through the wide and narrow sides (A and B) into the edges of the top (C). Use 1⅝-inch screws spaced about 5 inches apart.

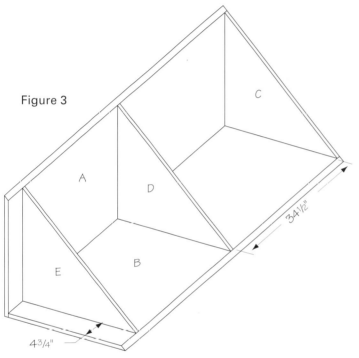

Figure 3

8. Repeat the procedure in step 7 to attach the shelf (D) 34½ inches below the top (C).

9. Again repeat the procedure in step 7 to attach the bottom (E) 4¾ inches from the bottom edges of the wide and narrow sides (A and B).

ADDING THE TRIM

10. Carefully measure across the bottom of the cupboard. Add 1½ inches to that measurement and cut one bottom trim (F) from 1 x 6 pine to the new measurement.

11. Miter both ends of the bottom trim (F) at opposing 45-degree angles, as shown in figure 4.

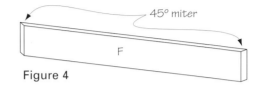

45° miter

F

Figure 4

12. Apply glue to the meeting surfaces, and fit the bottom trim (F) over the edge of the bottom (E), as shown in figure 5. Screw through the bottom trim (F) into the edge of the bottom (E) and the edges of the wide and narrow sides (A and B), using 1⅝-inch screws spaced about 5 inches apart.

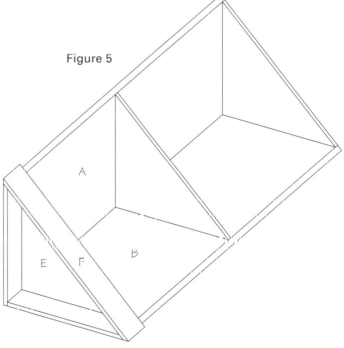

Figure 5

13. To provide support for the front beaded trim, 2 x 2 strips (G) must be attached to both top (C) and the shelf (D). Refer to figure 6 to measure and cut 2 x 2 strips for the underside of the top (C) and shelf (D). Both ends of each of the two strips (G) must be mitered at opposing 45-degree angles. Apply glue to the meeting surfaces, and nail the strips (G) in place, using 1¼-inch (3d) finish nails spaced about every 4 inches.

15. Measure and cut the beveled strips (H) to fit between the top (C), shelf (D), and bottom (E), as shown in figure 8. Apply glue to the meeting surfaces, and nail them in place using 1¼-inch (3d) finish nails spaced about every 4 inches.

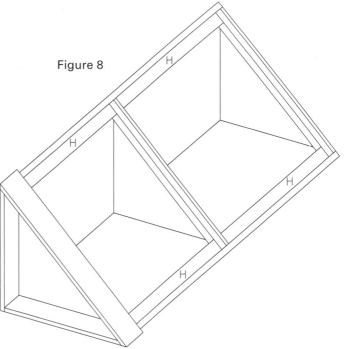

Figure 8

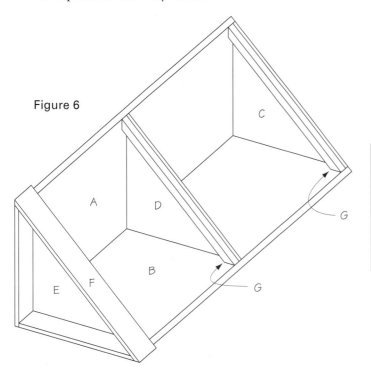

Figure 6

14. The plywood edges on the wide and narrow sides (A and B) must also be supported by 2 x 2 strips (H). Bevel a total of 12 linear feet of 2 x 2 strips (H) at a 45-degree angle, as shown in figure 7.

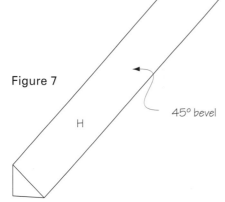

Figure 7

45° bevel

H

16. Refer to the project photograph to place the remaining trim on the corner cupboard. Begin by attaching the four decorative squares (I) at the two sides of the top (C) and the shelf (D). The position of the decorative squares (I) is a little bit tricky. The beaded molding (which you will add in the next step) is only 3 inches wide, whereas the decorative squares (I) are 4 inches wide. So the decorative squares (I) must be positioned so that the beaded molding is centered on all sides of the decorative squares, as illustrated in figure 9. Measure carefully and glue and nail the four decorative squares (I) in their positions. Use two or three 1½-inch (4d) finish nails through each of the decorative squares (I).

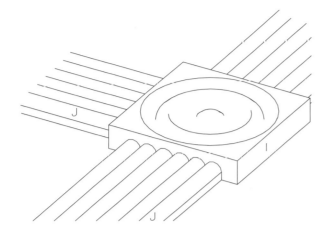

17. Again refer to the photograph for placement of the beaded trim (J). Measure and cut each of the six pieces to cover both sides, the top, and the shelf front. Apply glue to the meeting surfaces, and nail through the beaded trim (J), using four or five 1¼-inch (3d) finish nails on each piece.

FINISHING

18. Fill the screw holes, crevices, and cracks with wood filler.

19. Sand all surfaces of the completed cupboard.

20. Stain or paint the cupboard the color of your choice. We painted the front trim pieces with a metallic bronze paint and left the remainder of the cupboard its natural color. Then we sealed the entire cupboard with a gloss polyurethane.

Fireplace Screen

This screen was actually designed for my neighbor. She had a see-through fireplace from the living room to the guest bedroom and needed a privacy screen. Wouldn't you know it, ever since she installed it in her guest bedroom, we've been turning out different versions for all our friends. We added pink flowers to coordinate with her bedroom, but have also made them with bay leaves, ceramic tile pieces, and even miniature dolls.

Materials

- 12 linear feet of 1 x 12 pine

Hardware and Supplies:

- 6 2½-inch-long brass hinges
- 1 quart of textured sand finish (the type used for ceilings and walls)

Cutting List

Code	Description	Qty	Materials	Dimensions
A	Panels	4	1 x 12 pine	31" long

CONSTRUCTING THE SCREEN

1. Cut four panels (A) from 1 x 12 pine, each measuring 31 inches long.

2. Round the end of one panel (A), as shown in figure 1. The exact shape is not critical. We used an ordinary household plate to trace the curve onto the board. Make certain that the curve is centered on the board, so that the sides are equal in length.

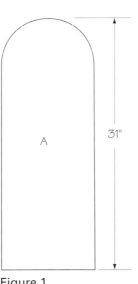

A

31"

Figure 1

3. Use the rounded first panel (A) as a pattern to cut the three remaining panels.

4. Sand all four of the panels (A) thoroughly.

FINISHING

5. Wipe the texture on all surfaces of each of the panels (A). Then use a sponge to lightly dab over the entire texture. If you place the panel (A) on top of paint cans, you can texture the first side and all of the edges. When that has dried, turn the panel over and texture the remaining side.

6. To match the decor in the bedroom where we placed the fireplace screen, we added pink flowers to our panels. You can use autumn leaves, bay leaves, or any other item that coordinates with your room. Simply dip one side of the item in the texture and apply it to the panel. When the texture dries, the item will be permanently attached.

7. Follow the manufacturer's directions to install two hinges between each of the panels, as shown in the photograph. Take care that you leave enough room between the panels so that they do not rub together and that the entire assembly is completely even along the bottom edges.

Entertainment Center

If you have always wanted a good-looking entertainment center to house your stereo, television, records, CDs, and books, here's the answer. You can build it for much less than you would pay in a furniture store. This one is built in three individual sections so that it can be moved easily. We sponge-painted ours and are very happy with the finished project.

Materials

The materials specified are enough to make two outer cabinets and one center cabinet.

- 27 linear feet of 1 x 2 pine
- 150 linear feet of 1 x 4 pine
- 36 linear feet of 2 x 4 pine
- 3 linear feet of 1 x 8 pine
- 17 linear feet of 5½" crown molding
- 13 linear feet of 3" crown molding
- 24 linear feet of ¾" rope molding
- 7½ sheets (4' x 8') of ¾" plywood
- 4½ sheets (4' x 8') of ¼" plywood

Hardware

- 325 ¾" wire brads
- 250 1" (2d) nails
- 20 1¼" (3d) nails
- 350 1½" screws
- 36 2" screws
- 24 2½" screws
- 24 3" screws
- 16 cabinet door hinges
- 8 door pulls
- 8 magnetic catches

Special Tools and Techniques

- Router
- Pipe clamps or long bar clamps
- Staple gun
- Miters

Cutting List

Code	Description	Qty	Materials	Dimensions
A	Sides	2	¾" plywood	23¼" x 82½"
B	Top/Bottom	2	¾" plywood	23¼" x 37½"
C	Shelf	4	¾" plywood	23¼" x 36"
D	Vertical Trim	2	1 x 4 pine	84" long
E	Horizontal Trim	2	1 x 4 pine	30½" long
F	Wide Horizontal Trim	1	1 x 8 pine	30½" long
G	Molding Trim	1	¾" rope molding	30½" long
H	Top/Bottom Door Trim	8	1 x 4 pine	15" long
I	Wide Side Door Trim	4	1 x 4 pine	38" long
J	Narrow Side Door Trim	4	1 x 2 pine	38" long
K	Door Panel	4	¼" plywood	14¾" x 34½"
L	Support Blocks	2	1 x 2 pine	4" long
M	Base Sides	2	2 x 4 pine	18½" long
N	Base Front/Back	2	2 x 4 pine	35" long
O	Base Supports	4	2 x 4 pine	12" long
P	Back	1	¼" plywood	37½" x 84"
Q	Sides	4	¾" plywood	16" x 78½"

Code	Description	Qty	Materials	Dimensions
R	Top/Bottom	4	¾" plywood	16" x 30"
S	Shelf	10	¾" plywood	16" x 28½"
T	Vertical Trim	4	1 x 4 pine	80" long
U	Horizontal Trim	8	1 x 4 pine	23" long
V	Molding Trim	2	¾" rope molding	23" long
W	Top/Bottom Door Trim	8	1 x 4 pine	11½" long
X	Wide Side Door Trim	4	1 x 4 pine	32½" long
Y	Narrow Side Door Trim	4	1 x 2 pine	32½"
Z	Door Panel	4	¼" plywood	11¼" x 29"
AA	Support Blocks	8	1 x 2 pine	4" long
BB	Base Sides	4	2 x 4 pine	11" long
CC	Base Front/Back	4	2 x 4 pine	28" long
DD	Base Supports	8	2 x 4 pine	7½" long
EE	Back	2	¼" plywood	30" x 80"
FF	Top Molding	(5½" crown molding)		cut to fit
GG	Rope Molding	(¾" rope molding)		cut to fit
HH	Bottom Molding	(3" crown molding)		cut to fit

CONSTRUCTING THE CENTER CABINET

1. Cut two sides (A) from ¾-inch plywood, each measuring 23¼ x 82½ inches.

2. Cut two top/bottoms (B) from ¾-inch plywood, each measuring 23¼ x 37½ inches.

3. Place the two sides (A) on edge on a level surface, 36 inches apart. Fit the top/bottoms (B) over the ends of the sides (A) to form a rectangle, measuring 37½ x 84 inches, as shown in figure 1. Apply glue to the meeting surfaces, and screw through the top/bottoms (B) into the edges of the sides (A). Use 1½-inch screws spaced about every 5 inches.

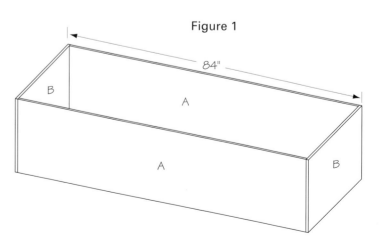

Figure 1

84"

B

A

A

B

4. Cut four shelves (C) from ¾-inch plywood, each measuring 23¼ x 36 inches.

5. Place the first shelf (C) 2 inches below the top (B). Screw through the sides (A) into the edges of the shelf (C), as shown in figure 2. Use 1½-inch screws spaced about every 5 inches.

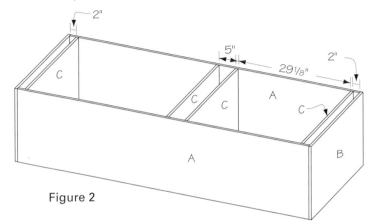

Figure 2

6. Repeat the procedure in step 5 to attach the second shelf (C) 29⅛ inches below the first one.

7. Attach the third shelf (C) 5 inches below the second one.

8. Attach the fourth shelf (C) 2 inches above the bottom (B).

ADDING THE TRIM TO THE CENTER CABINET

9. Cut two vertical trims (D) from 1 x 4 pine, each measuring 84 inches long.

10. Apply glue to the meeting surfaces, and screw one vertical trim (D) to the edge of one side (A), as shown in figure 3. Use 1½-inch screws spaced about every 5 inches.

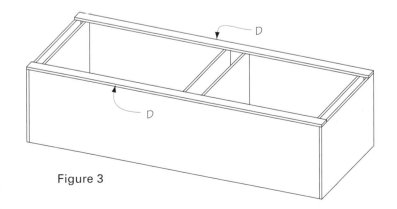

Figure 3

11. Repeat step 10 to attach the remaining vertical trim (D) to the opposite side (A).

12. Cut two horizontal trims (E) from 1 x 4 pine, each measuring 30½ inches long.

13. Apply glue to the plywood edges, and attach one horizontal trim (E) over the edges of the top (B) and the first shelf (C), as shown in figure 4. Screw through the horizontal trim (E) into the edges of the top (B) and shelf (C), using 1½-inch screws about every 6 inches.

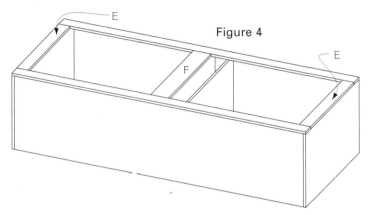

Figure 4

14. Repeat step 13 to attach the second horizontal trim (E) to the fourth shelf (C) and the bottom (B).

15. Cut one wide horizontal trim (F) from 1 x 8 pine, measuring 30½ inches long.

16. Attach the wide horizontal trim (F) flush with the upper surface of the third shelf (C). Apply glue to the plywood edge and screw through the wide horizontal trim (F) into the edge of the third shelf (C). Use 1½-inch screws placed about 6 inches apart.

17. Cut one molding trim (G) from ¾-inch rope molding, measuring 30½ inches long.

18. Apply glue to the molding trim (G), and nail it over the exposed edge of the second shelf (C) using 1-inch (2d) nails spaced about every 5 inches.

MAKING THE DOORS FOR THE CENTER CABINET

19. Cut eight top/bottom door trims (H) from 1 x 4 pine, each measuring 15 inches long.

20. Miter one end of each of the eight top/bottom door trims (H) at a 45-degree angle, as shown in figure 5.

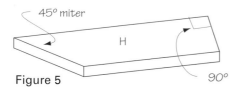

Figure 5

21. Cut four wide side door trims (I) from 1 x 4 pine, each measuring 38 inches long.

22. Miter each of the four wide side door trims (I) at opposing 45-degree angles, as shown in figure 6.

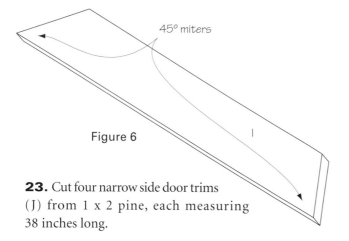

Figure 6

23. Cut four narrow side door trims (J) from 1 x 2 pine, each measuring 38 inches long.

24. Cut four door panels (K) from ¼-inch plywood, measuring 14¾ x 34½ inches.

25. Place two top/bottom door trims (H), face down, 31 inches apart, and parallel to each other. The miters should oppose each other, as shown in figure 7.

26. Fit one wide side door trim (I) between the two top/bottom door trims (H), as shown in figure 7.

27. Place one narrow door trim (J) against the flat ends of the two top/bottom door trims (H), as shown in figure 7.

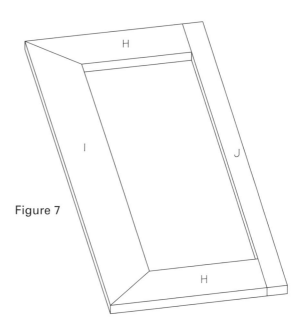

Figure 7

28. Apply glue to the meeting surfaces, and clamp the four pieces together for several hours.

29. Repeat steps 25 through 28 three more times using the remaining six top/bottom door trims (H), three wide side door trims (I), and three narrow side door trims (J).

30. The next step is optional. We routed both the inside and outside edges of the front of the assembled door trims (H, I, and J) using a round-over bit. Before routing, we temporarily added extra support to the four glued joints by stapling across each joint using a staple gun. After the routing was complete, we removed the staples.

31. Place a routed trim assembly (routed side down) on a flat surface. Place a door panel (K) over the assembly, flush with the outer edge of the narrow side door trim (J), as shown in figure 8. The other three trim pieces (H and I) should be exposed by 1¾ inches. Apply glue to the meeting surfaces, and nail through the door panel (K) into each of the four trim pieces (H, I, and J), using small ¾-inch brads, placed about every 4 inches.

32. Repeat step 31 three more times to complete the remaining three cabinet doors.

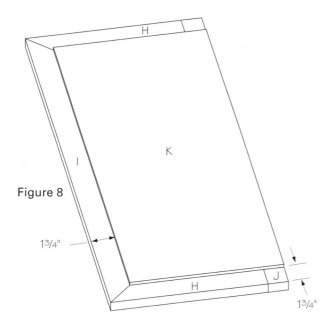

Figure 8

13/4"

13/4"

H

I

K

H

J

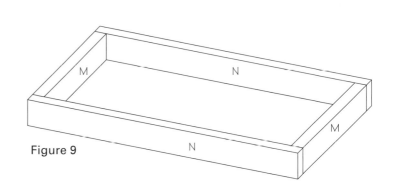

Figure 9

M

N

M

N

FINISHING THE CENTER CABINET

33. Cut two support blocks (L) from 1 x 2 pine, each measuring 4 inches long.

34. Place the completed cabinet on its front. Apply glue to the meeting surfaces, and nail each of the support blocks (K) over the two joints between the vertical trims (D) and the wide horizontal trim (F), flush with the lower edge of the wide horizontal trim (F). Nail through each support block (L), using two 1¼-inch (3d) finish nails, one on each side of the joint.

35. Cut two base sides (M) from 2 x 4 pine, each measuring 18½ inches long.

36. Cut two base front/backs (N) from 2 x 4 pine, each measuring 35 inches long.

37. Place the two base sides (M) parallel to each other and 32 inches apart. Fit the two base front/backs (N) over the base sides (M), to form a rectangle measuring 35 x 21½ inches, as shown in figure 9. Screw through the base front/backs (N) into the base sides (M) using two 2½-inch screws on each joint.

38. Cut four base supports (O) from 2 x 4 pine, each measuring 12 inches long.

39. Miter the ends of each base support (O) across the width at opposing 45-degree angles, as shown in figure 10.

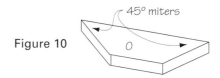

45° miters

Figure 10

O

40. Place the base assembly on a perfectly level surface. Apply glue to the mitered ends, and screw a base support (O) into each of the four corners of the base assembly, as shown in figure 11. The base supports (O) should be flush with what will be the top of the base assembly. Use two 3-inch screws on each of the base supports (O).

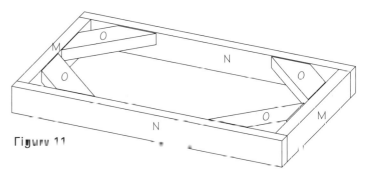

O

M

O

N

O

N

M

Figure 11

41. Center the base assembly on the bottom of the cabinet, with the base supports (O) meeting the cabinet bottom (B). The base assembly should be 1¼ inches from each of the edges of the cabinet bottom (B) and the front of the bottom horizontal trim (E). Apply glue to the top of the base assembly, and screw through the base supports (O) into the cabinet bottom (B) using three 2-inch screws on each base support (N).

42. Cut one back (P) from ¼-inch plywood, measuring 84 x 37½ inches.

43. Place the back (P) over the back of the cabinet, overlapping the sides (A) and top/bottoms (B). Apply glue to the meeting surfaces, and nail through the back (P) into the edges of the sides (A) and top/bottoms (B), using 1-inch (2d) finish nails spaced every 4 inches.

44. Turn the completed cabinet on its back and place the four cabinet doors over the front openings in the cabinet. Allow about ⅛-inch space between each pair of doors. Check to make certain that the doors are straight and that the door panels (K) fit evenly inside each of the openings in the cabinet assembly. Then attach the doors to the cabinet using two hinges on each door. Also install door catches on each of the cabinet doors to make certain that they will stay closed when you shut them.

45. The top and bottom crown moldings will be added later after all three cabinets are finished.

CONSTRUCTING THE OUTER CABINETS

The instructions here are for one outer cabinet. Obviously, two cabinets must be built to complete the entertainment center. You may wish to cut the pieces for the second outer cabinet at the same time as you cut those for the first. This saves time and insures that both cabinets will be the same. The Cutting List shows the quantities needed for both cabinets.

46. Cut two sides (Q) from ¾-inch plywood, each measuring 16 x 78½ inches.

47. Cut two top/bottoms (R) from ¾-inch plywood, each measuring 16 x 30 inches.

48. Place the two sides (Q) on edge on a level surface, 28½ inches apart. Fit the top/bottoms (R) over the ends of the sides (Q) to form a rectangle measuring 30 x 80 inches, as shown in figure 12. Apply glue to the meeting surfaces, and screw through the top/bottoms (R) into the edges of the sides (Q). Use 1½-inch screws spaced about every 5 inches.

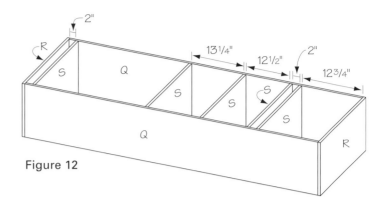

Figure 12

49. Cut five shelves (S) from ¾-inch plywood, each measuring 16 x 28½ inches.

50. Place the first shelf (S) 12¾ inches below the top (R). Screw through the sides (Q) into the edges of the shelf (S), as shown in figure 12. Use 1½-inch screws spaced about every 5 inches.

51. Repeat the procedure in step 50 to attach the second shelf (S) 2 inches below the first one.

52. Attach the third shelf (S) 12½ inches below the second one.

53. Attach the fourth shelf (S) 13¼ inches below the third one.

54. Attach the fifth shelf (S) 2 inches above the bottom (R).

ADDING THE TRIM TO THE OUTER CABINETS

55. Cut two vertical trims (T) from 1 x 4 pine, each measuring 80 inches long.

56. Apply glue to the meeting surfaces, and screw one vertical trim (T) to the edge of one side (Q), as shown in figure 13. Use 1½-inch screws spaced about every 5 inches.

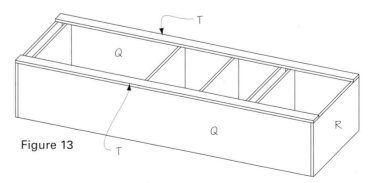

Figure 13

57. Repeat step 56 to attach the remaining vertical trim (T) to the opposite side (Q).

58. Cut four horizontal trims (U) from 1 x 4 pine, each measuring 23 inches.

59. Apply glue to the plywood edge, and attach one horizontal trim (U) over the edge of the top (R), as shown in figure 14. Screw through the horizontal trim (U) into the edge of the top (R), using 1½-inch screws about every 6 inches.

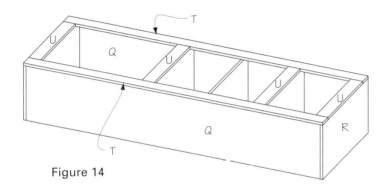

Figure 14

60. Repeat step 59 to attach the second horizontal trim (U) over the edges of the first and second shelves (S).

61. Attach the third horizontal trim (U) flush with the top surface of the fourth shelf (S).

62. Attach the fourth horizontal trim (U) over the edges of the fifth shelf (S) and the bottom (R).

63. Cut one molding trim (V) from ¾-inch-wide rope molding, measuring 23 inches long.

64. Apply glue to the meeting surfaces, and nail the molding trim (V) over the exposed edge of the third shelf (S). Nail it in place using 1-inch (2d) finish nails spaced about every 5 inches.

MAKING THE CABINET DOORS FOR THE OUTER CABINETS

65. Cut four top/bottom door trims (W) from 1 x 4 pine, each measuring 11½ inches long.

66. Miter one end of each of the four top/bottom door trims (W) at a 45-degree angle, as shown in figure 5.

67. Cut two wide side door trims (X) from 1 x 4 pine, each measuring 32½ inches long.

68. Miter each of the two wide side door trims (X) at opposing 45-degree angles, as shown in figure 6.

69. Cut four narrow side door trims (Y) from 1 x 2 pine, each measuring 32½ inches long.

70. Cut four door panels (Z) from ¼-inch plywood, measuring 11¼ x 29 inches.

71. Place two top/bottom door trims (W), face down, 25½ inches apart, and parallel to each other. The miters should oppose each other, as shown in figure 7.

72. Fit one wide side door trim (X) between the two top/bottom door trims (W), as shown in figure 7.

73. Place one narrow door trim (Y) against the flat ends of the two top/bottom door trims (W), as shown in figure 7.

74. Apply glue to the meeting surfaces, and clamp the four pieces together for several hours.

75. Repeat steps 71 through 74, using the remaining two top/bottom door trims (W), wide side door trim (X), and narrow side door trim (Y).

76. The next step is optional. We routed both the inside and outside edges of the front of the assembled door trims (W, X, and Y) using a round-over bit. Before routing, we temporarily added extra support to the four glued joints by stapling across each joint using a staple gun. After the routing was complete, we removed the staples.

77. Place a routed trim assembly (routed side down) on a flat surface. Place a door panel (Z) over the assembly, flush with the outer edge of the narrow side door trim (Y), as shown in figure 8. The other three trim pieces (W and X) should be exposed by 1¾ inches. Apply glue to the meeting surfaces, and nail through the door panel (Z) into the each of the four trim pieces (W, X, and Y), using small ¾-inch brads, placed about every 4 inches.

78. Repeat step 77 to complete the other cabinet door.

FINISHING THE OUTER CABINET

79. Cut four support blocks (AA) from 1 x 2 pine, each measuring 4 inches long.

80. Place the completed cabinet on its front. Apply glue to the meeting surfaces and nail each of the support blocks (AA) over the four exposed joints between the vertical trims (T) and the horizontal trims (U). Nail through each support block (AA), using two 1¼-inch (3d) finish nails, one on each side of the joint.

81. Cut two base sides (BB) from 2 x 4 pine, each measuring 11 inches long.

82. Cut two base front/backs (CC) from 2 x 4 pine, each measuring 28 inches long.

83. Place the two base sides (BB) parallel to each other and 25 inches apart. Fit the two base front/backs (CC) over the base sides (BB), to form a rectangle measuring 28 x 14 inches, as shown in figure 9. Screw through the base front/back (CC) into the base sides (BB), using two 2½-inch screws on each joint.

84. Cut four base supports (DD) from 2 x 4 pine, each measuring 7½ inches long.

85. Miter the ends of each base support (DD) across the width at opposing 45-degree angles, as shown in figure 10.

86. Place the base assembly on a perfectly level surface. Apply glue to the meeting surfaces, and screw a base support (DD) into each of the four corners of the base assem-

bly, flush with what will be the top of the base assembly, as shown in figure 11. Use two 3-inch screws on each of the base supports (DD).

87. Center the base assembly on the bottom of the cabinet with the base supports (DD) meeting the cabinet bottom (R). The base assembly should be 1 inch from each of the edges of the cabinet bottom (R). Apply glue to the meeting surfaces, and screw through the base supports (DD) into the cabinet bottom (R), using three 2-inch screws on each base support (DD).

88. Cut one back (EE) from ¼-inch plywood, measuring 80 x 30 inches.

89. Place the back (EE) over the back of the cabinet, overlapping the sides (Q) and top/bottoms (R). Apply glue to the meeting surfaces, and nail through the back (EE) into the edges of the sides (Q) and top/bottoms (R) using 1-inch (2d) finish nails spaced every 4 inches.

90. Turn the completed cabinet on its back and place the two cabinet doors over the lower opening in the cabinet. Allow about ⅛-inch space between the doors. Check to make certain that the doors are straight and that the door panels (Z) fit evenly inside the opening in the cabinet assembly. Then attach the doors to the cabinet using two hinges on each door. Also install door catches on each of the cabinet doors to make certain that they will stay closed when you shut them.

91. The top and bottom crown molding will be added later after all three cabinets are finished.

92. Take a deep breath, admire your handiwork—and make another outer cabinet!

FINISHING THE ENTERTAINMENT CENTER

93. Fill the screw holes, crevices, and cracks with wood filler.

94. Sand all surfaces of all three of the completed cabinets.

95. Place the three cabinets together on a level surface. To hold the three cabinets together temporarily, insert two or three 1¼-inch screws through the inside of the center cabinet into the sides of each of the outer cabinets. Do not glue the cabinets together or you will be unable to move them through doors.

96. Refer to the project photograph for placement of the moldings. Carefully measure and cut 5½-inch-wide crown molding (FF) to fit around the top of the joined cabinets. The bottom of the top molding (FF) laps onto the top of the cabinets by only ¾ inch. If you are not skilled in cutting crown molding, refer to the "Tools, Techniques, and Materials" section for assistance. Use glue and 1-inch (2d) finish nails to attach the molding to the individual cabinets. *Do not use glue on the molding joints between the cabinets.*

97. Carefully measure and cut rope molding (GG) and attach it to the installed crown molding, as shown in the photograph.

98. Again, refer to the project photograph. Carefully measure and cut 3-inch-wide crown molding (HH) to fit around the bottom of each of the cabinets. The top of the bottom molding (HH) laps over the bottom of the cabinet by only ¾ inch. Use glue and 1-inch (2d) finish nails to attach the molding to the individual cabinets. *Do not use glue on the molding joints between the cabinets.*

99. Stain or paint the entertainment center the color of your choice. We first painted ours with a bright white paint and then sponge-painted it with an almond paint. We then sealed it with a clear polyurethane.

End Table

This simple-to-build end table is perfect for spaces next to a couch that won't accommodate a larger table. It's large enough to accommodate a lamp and books, but small enough to walk around without permanent injury to your shins. We finished our table in a dark stain to coordinate with our couch, but left the decorative trim its natural color.

Materials

- 22 linear feet of 1 x 4 pine
- 2 linear feet of 1 x 12 pine
- 7 linear feet of ¾-inch rope molding

Hardware

- 15 1¼" (3d) nails
- 16 1¼" screws
- 44 1½" screws

Cutting List

Code	Description	Qty	Materials	Dimensions
A	Top	1	1 x 12 pine	20½" long
B	Front/Back	2	1 x 4 pine	20½" long
C	Sides	2	1 x 4 pine	12¾" long
D	Wide Leg	4	1 x 4 pine	22½" long
E	Narrow Leg	4	1 x 4 pine, ripped	22½" long
F	Rope Molding	4	¾" wide	cut to fit

BUILDING THE TABLE TOP

1. Cut one top (A) from 1 x 12 pine, measuring 20½ inches long.

2. Cut two front/backs (B) from 1 x 4 pine, each measuring 20½ inches long.

3. Cut two sides (C) from 1 x 4 pine, each measuring 12¾ inches long.

4. Place the top (A) on a level surface. Place the two front/backs (B) on edge on either side of the top (A), matching the 20½-inch-long sides, as shown in figure 1. Apply glue to the long edges of the top (A), and screw through the front/backs (B) into the edges of the top (A), using five evenly spaced 1½-inch screws on each joint. This joint can also be glued and clamped for an hour or so, omitting the screws.

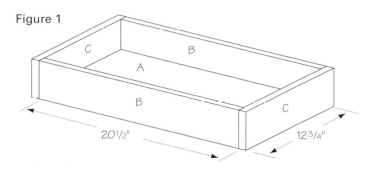

Figure 1

20½"   12¾"

5. Place the two sides (C) over the ends of the two front/backs (B), as shown in figure 1. Screw through the sides (C) into the ends of the front/backs (B) and the top (A), using two or three 1½-inch screws on each joint.

MAKING THE LEGS

6. Cut four wide legs (D) from 1 x 4 pine, each measuring 22½ inches long.

7. Rip a total of 8 feet of 1 x 4 pine to a width of 2¾ inches.

8. Cut four narrow legs (E) from the 2¾-inch-wide ripped material, each measuring 22½ inches long.

9. Attach one narrow leg (E) to one wide leg (D) as shown in figure 2. Apply glue to the edge of the narrow leg (E), and screw through the wide leg (D) into the edge of the narrow leg (E), using five evenly spaced 1½-inch screws. This joint can also be glued and clamped for an hour or so, omitting the screws. The finished leg assembly should measure 3½ inches on each of the outside widths.

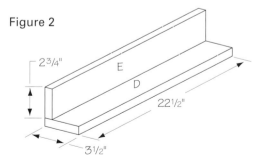

Figure 2

2¾"   E   D   22½"   3½"

10. Repeat step 4 three more times, using the remaining three narrow legs (E) and three wide legs (D).

11. Place the base assembly (A and B) on a level surface. Attach the four leg assemblies to each of the four corners of the base assembly, as shown in figure 3. Apply glue to the meeting surfaces, and screw through both sides of each leg assembly, using two 1¼-inch screws on each side. After driving each screw, use a try square to make sure that the legs (D) remain at a right angle to both front (A) and side (C).

12. Measure carefully and cut pieces of ¾-inch-wide rope molding (F) to fit around the completed end table over the front, back, and sides, mitering the molding at each of the four corners, as shown in the photograph. Attach the molding to the end table, using glue and 1¼-inch (3d) nails spaced every 4 inches.

FINISHING

13. Fill any screw holes or imperfections in the wood with wood filler.

14. Thoroughly sand all of the wood parts on the completed end table.

15. Stain or paint the table the color of your choice. We chose a deep green stain to coordinate with our sofa, but left the rope molding its natural color for contrast.

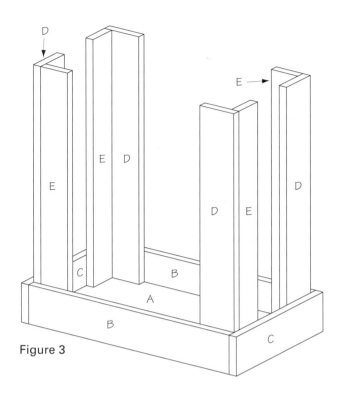

Figure 3

With the projects in the first three sections of this book, Mark and I have filled our kitchen, dining room, and living room with furniture. At the same time, we've created a unified and functional common area in our house.

The rooms look unified because all of our pieces are designed in a similar scale, made of similar materials, and finished with similar techniques and colors. This photograph contains seven projects made with plans from this book, and the entire living area flows together as if professionally decorated.

This blending isn't accidental. We used key details to refer from one furniture design to another. For example, we used the same proportions in the dining table and in the coffee table, right down to the cannonball-style legs.

In the end table, we picked up the green from the buffet's columns, and we used the same rope molding as we did in the entertainment center. We even used the same sponge-painting technique on the entertainment center and on the coffee table to help unify the living room. At the same time, the distinctive touches we added (such as the tiled surface of the coffee table) keep the overall effect from becoming monotonous. Details are important!

Daybed

How do you combine an office and a guest bedroom? Build this good-looking daybed. During office hours it provides ample seating, and when an overnight guest arrives, it accommodates them in style. Even spare sheets and blankets are kept handy: the front panels are hinged to provide under-the-bed storage.

Materials

- 12 linear feet of 1 x 2 pine
- 110 linear feet of 1 x 4 pine
- 6 linear feet of 1 x 12 pine
- 86 linear feet of 2 x 4 pine
- 1 piece of ¾" plywood, 35" x 74"

Hardware

- 200 1¼" (3d) nails
- 24 2" (6d) nails
- 30 1½" wood screws
- 63 2" wood screws
- 102 2½" wood screws
- 4 cabinet hinges
- 4 magnetic catches

Special Tools and Techniques

- Bar clamps or pipe clamps
- Miters
- Dadoes
- Hand plane
- Router with ⅜" round-over cutter

Cutting List

Code	Description	Qty	Materials	Dimensions
A	Long Frame	4	2 x 4 pine	74" long
B	Short Frame	4	2 x 4 pine	35" long
C	Frame Support	6	2 x 4 pine	28" long
D	Frame Connector	10	2 x 4 pine	11¼" long
E	Platform	1	¾" plywood	35" x 74"
F	Headboard Top/Bottom	2	2 x 4 pine	35" long
G	Headboard Slat	10	1 x 4 pine	35" long
H	Headboard Side	1	1 x 2 pine	41" long

Cutting List, continued

Code	Description	Qty	Materials	Dimensions
I	Footboard Top/Bottom	2	2 x 4 pine	35" long
J	Footboard Slat	10	1 x 4 pine	9¼" long
K	Footboard Side	2	1 x 2 pine	15¼" long
L	Bottom Back	1	2 x 4 pine	75½" long
M	Long Top Back	1	2 x 4 pine	40" long
N	Short Top Back	1	2 x 4 pine	39" long
O	Back Connector	1	2 x 4 pine	15½" long
P	Long Back Slat	11	1 x 4 pine	35" long
Q	Short Back Slat	11	1 x 4 pine	23" long
R	Long Back Side	1	1 x 2 pine	41" long
S	Short Back Side	1	1 x 2 pine	29" long
T	Horizontal Trim	2	1 x 4 pine	74" long
U	Vertical Trim	3	1 x 4 pine	8¼" long
V	Storage Fronts	2	1 x 12 pine	33¾" long

MAKING THE BASE STRUCTURE

1. Cut four long frames (A) from 2 x 4 pine, each measuring 74 inches long.

2. Miter the ends of each of the four long frames (A) at opposing 45-degree angles, as shown in figure 1.

3. Cut four short frames (B) from 2 x 4 pine, each measuring 35 inches long.

4. Miter the ends of each of the four short frames (B) at opposing 45-degree angles, as shown in figure 1.

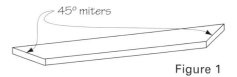

45° miters

Figure 1

5. Place two short frames (B) on a level surface, parallel to each other and 67 inches apart.

6. Fit two long frames (A) between the two short frames (B) to form a rectangle measuring 35 x 74 inches, as shown in figure 2. Apply glue to the mitered surfaces, and fasten each joint with two 2½-inch screws driven from the outside edge across the miter joint, one on each side.

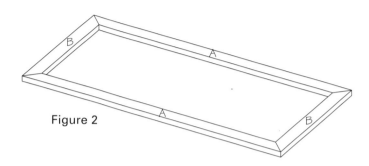

Figure 2

7. Repeat step 6 to construct a second 35 x 67-inch rectangular frame using the remaining two long frames (A) and two short frames (B).

8. Cut six frame supports (C) from 2 x 4 pine, each measuring 28 inches long.

9. Place three frame supports (C), evenly spaced, inside one rectangular frame, as shown in figure 3. Toenail the three frame supports (C) in place, using two 2-inch (6d) finish nails on each joint.

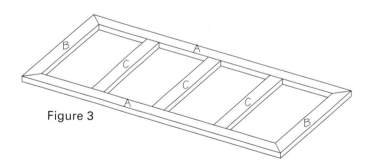

Figure 3

10. Repeat step 10 to add the remaining three frame supports (C) to the other rectangular frame.

11. Cut ten frame connectors (D) from 2 x 4 pine, each measuring 11¼ inches long.

12. This next step will require a helping hand from an interested bystander. Place one rectangular frame on a level surface. Place each of the ten frame connectors (C) on top of the frame, as shown in figure 4. Note that each corner of the frame has two connectors (D) and each long side of the frame has a frame connector (D) in the middle. Each of the frame connectors (D) must be flush with the outer edge of the rectangular frame. Then place the second frame on top of the ten frame connectors (D). Measure to make sure that the frame connectors (D) are correctly positioned on the second frame. Have your assistant steady the assembly while you screw through the second rectangular frame into each of the ten frame connectors (D). Use two 2½-inch screws on each joint.

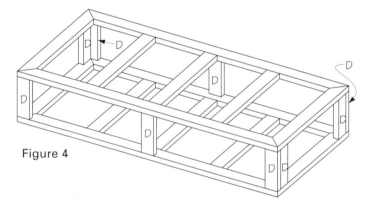

Figure 4

13. Where two frame connectors (D) meet in each of the four corners, screw through the overlapping frame connector (D) into the meeting edge of the other frame connector (D). Use three 2½-inch screws on each joint.

14. Turn the entire assembly upside down, replace the first rectangular frame on the top, measure to check for proper placement, and again screw through the rectangular frame into the frame connectors (D).

15. Cut one platform (E) from ¾-inch plywood, measuring 35 x 74 inches.

16. Place the platform (E) over the assembly, as shown in figure 5. Apply glue, and screw through the platform (D) into the long frame (A), short frame (B), and each of the three frame supports (E). Use 2-inch screws spaced about every 5 inches.

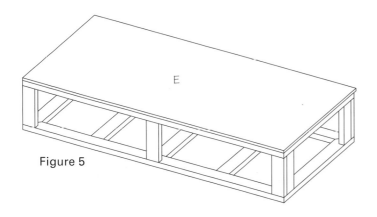

Figure 5

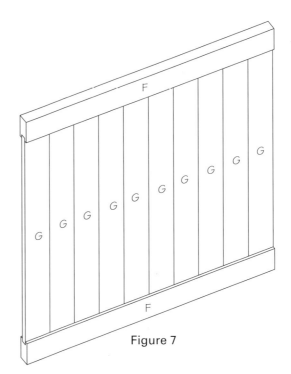

Figure 7

MAKING THE HEADBOARD

17. Cut two headboard top/bottoms (F) from 2 x 4 pine, each measuring 35 inches long.

18. Cut a ¾-inch-wide dado ½-inch deep down the length of one edge of each of the headboard top/bottoms (F), as shown in figure 6.

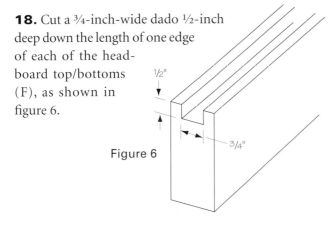

½"

¾"

Figure 6

19. Cut ten headboard slats (G) from 1 x 4 pine, each measuring 35 inches long.

20. Working on a level surface, place the two headboard top/bottoms (F) parallel to each other, with the dadoes to the inside, as shown in figure 7. Fit the ends of the ten headboard slats (G) into the dadoes in the headboard top/bottoms (F). When the headboard slats are properly fitted, the distance between the two headboard top/bottoms (F) should measure 34 inches. When the positions are perfect, the overall measurement of the headboard assembly should be 41 inches high and 35 inches long. Secure the headboard slats (G) by nailing through the back of the dadoed edge of the headboard top/bottoms (F) into the ends of the headboard slats (G) using two 1¼-inch (3d) finish nails on each joint.

21. Cut one headboard side (H) from 1 x 2 pine, measuring 41 inches long.

22. Apply glue to the edge of the end slat, and attach the headboard side (H) to one side of the headboard assembly, as shown in figure 8. Nail through the headboard side (H) into the ends of the headboard top/bottoms (F) and into the headboard slat (G). Use 1¼-inch (3d) finish nails spaced every 5 inches.

Figure 8

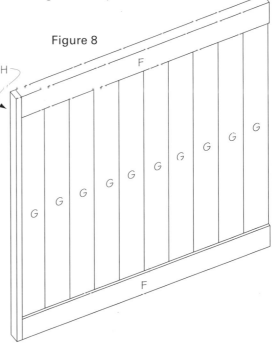

23. Attach the headboard to the head of the bed frame, as shown in figure 9. Note that the headboard assembly extends ¾ inch past the frame assembly at the front. To make the daybed portable in case of a move, do not use glue. Screw through the bottom of the assembly into the bottom base frame. Use 2½-inch screws spaced about every 6 inches. There will be a ⅜-inch gap between the headboard slats (G) and the edge of the platform (E).

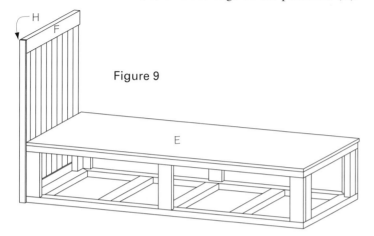

Figure 9

MAKING THE FOOTBOARD

24. Cut two footboard top/bottoms (G) from 2 x 4 pine, each measuring 35 inches long.

25. Cut a ¾-inch-wide dado ½-inch deep down the length of one edge of each of the footboard top/bottoms (I), as shown in figure 6.

26. Cut ten footboard slats (J) from 1 x 4 pine, each measuring 9¼ inches long.

27. Working on a level surface, place the two footboard top/bottoms (I) parallel to each other with the dadoes to the inside, as shown in figure 7. Fit the ends of the ten footboard slats (J) into the dadoes in the footboard top/bottoms (I). When the footboard slats are properly fitted, the distance between the two footboard top/bottoms should measure 8¼ inches. When the positions are perfect, the overall measurement of the footboard assembly should be 15¼ inches high and 35 inches long. Secure the footboard slats (J) by nailing through the dadoed edge of the footboard top/bottoms (I) into the ends of the footboard slats (I) using two 1¼-inch (3d) finish nails on each joint.

28. Cut one footboard side (K) from 1 x 2 pine measuring 15¼ inches long.

29. Attach the footboard side (K) to one side of the footboard assembly, in the same manner as shown in figure 8. Nail through the footboard side (K) into the ends of the footboard top/bottoms (I) and into the footboard slats (J). Use 1¼-inch (3d) finish nails spaced every 5 inches.

30. Attach the footboard assembly to the foot of the bed frame, as shown in figure 10. Note that the footboard assembly extends ¾ inch past the frame assembly at the front and ¼ inch above the platform (E). Apply glue to the meeting surfaces, and screw through the bottom of the footboard assembly into the bottom base frame. Also screw through the top of the footboard assembly into the top of the base frame. Use 2½-inch screws spaced about every 6 inches.

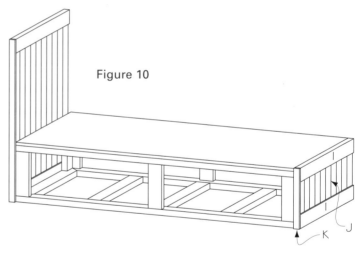

Figure 10

MAKING THE BACK

31. Cut one bottom back (L) from 2 x 4 pine, measuring 75½ inches long.

32. Cut one upper top back (M) from 2 x 4 pine, measuring 40 inches long.

33. Cut one lower top back (N) from 2 x 4 pine, measuring 39 inches long.

34. Cut one back connector (O) from 2 x 4 pine, measuring 15½ inches long.

35. Cut a ¾-inch-wide dado ½-inch deep down the length of one edge of the bottom back (L), the upper top back (M), the lower top back (N), and the back connector (O), as shown in figure 6.

36. Cut eleven long back slats (P) from 1 x 4 pine, each measuring 35 inches long.

37. Rip one long back slat (P) to a width of 2 inches.

38. Cut eleven short back slats (Q) from 1 x 4 pine, each measuring 23 inches long.

39. Note that the back of the daybed is two different heights. In order to connect the different heights, the upper top back (M) and the lower top back (N) must be mitered on one end, and the back connector (O) must be mitered on both ends. Refer to figure 11 and cut 45-degree miters on each of these three pieces. Make certain that the dadoed edge is on the lower side, as shown in the illustration.

Place the bottom back (L) on a level surface. Working from left to right, fit the ends of the eleven long back slats (P) into the bottom back (L), beginning with the 2-inch-wide back slat (P). Then fit the eleven short back slats (Q) into the same dado. Fit the long top back (M), the short top back (N), and the back connector (O) over the upper ends of the long and short back slats (P and Q). When the positions are perfect, the back assembly should measure 75½ inches long. Secure the long and short back slats (P and Q) by nailing through the dadoed edge of the bottom back (L), the upper top back (M), lower top back (N) and back connector (O) into the ends of the slats (P and Q), using two 1¼-inch (3d) finish nails on each joint.

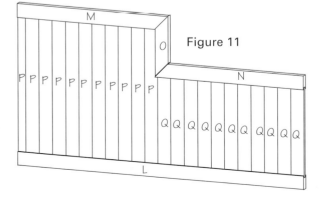

Figure 11

40. Cut one long back side (R) from 1 x 2 pine, measuring 41 inches long.

41. Apply glue to the edge of the 2-inch slat (P), and attach the long back side (R) to the long side of the back assembly, as shown in figure 12. Nail through the long back side (R) into the ends of the upper top back (M) and into the long back slat (P). Use 1¼-inch (3d) finish nails spaced every 5 inches.

42. Cut one short back side (S) from 1 x 2 pine, measuring 29 inches long.

43. Apply glue to the edge of the end slat (Q), and attach the short back side (S) to the short side of the back assembly, as shown in figure 12. Nail through the short back side (S) into the ends of the lower top back (N) and into the short back slat (Q). Use 1¼-inch (3d) finish nails spaced every 5 inches.

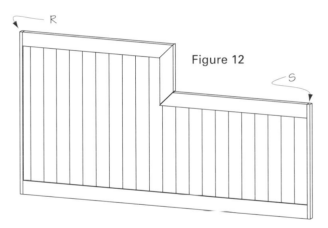

Figure 12

44. Attach the back assembly to the back of the bed frame, as shown in figure 13. Screw through the bottom of the back assembly into the bottom base frame. Also screw through the top of the back assembly into the top of the headboard assembly and through the short back side (S) into the top of the footboard assembly. Use 2½-inch screws spaced about every 6 inches.

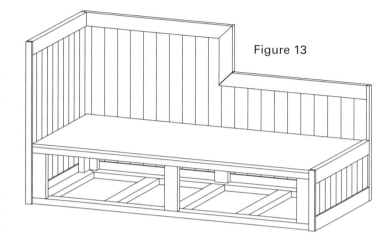

Figure 13

ADDING THE FRONT TRIM

45. Cut two horizontal trims (T) from 1 x 4 pine, each measuring 74 inches long.

46. Cut three vertical trims (U) from 1 x 4 pine, each measuring 8¼ inches long.

47. Attach one horizontal trim (T) between the headboard and the footboard flush with the bottom of the frame assembly, as shown in figure 14. Use glue and 1½-inch screws spaced about 6 inches apart.

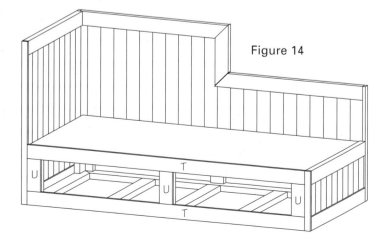

Figure 14

48. Attach each of the three vertical trims (U) to a front frame connector (D). Place the two outside vertical trims (U) against the headboard side (H) and the footboard side (K), respectively, but do not glue the vertical trim (U) to the headboard side (H). The third vertical trim (U) should be centered between the first two, as shown in figure 14. Apply glue to the meeting surfaces, and screw through each vertical trim (U) into its frame connector (D), using two 1½-inch screws.

49. Repeat step 48 to attach the remaining horizontal trim (T) between the headboard and footboard, against the tops of the vertical trims (U), as shown in figure 14. This horizontal trim (T) extends above the platform (E) by ¼ inch.

50. Cut two storage fronts (V) from 1 x 12 pine, each measuring 33¾ inches long.

51. Center the storage fronts (V), both vertically and horizontally, over the openings in the front of the completed daybed. Attach them to the daybed using two hinges on the bottom of each front. Install catches to keep the fronts closed. You may wish to round the front edges of the storage fronts (V) as we did.

FINISHING

52. Fill the screw holes, crevices, and cracks with wood filler.

53. Sand all surfaces of the completed daybed.

54. Stain or paint the daybed the color of your choice. We chose to retain the natural color of the pine and simply sealed it with a gloss polyurethane.

Desk

Our executive desk was built with specific needs in mind. We wanted a large desktop, large drawers, and a cubbyhole to house a roll-away hanging file cabinet. We are thrilled with our finished project. It's a beauty.

desk

Materials

- 55 linear feet of 1 x 4 pine
- 2 linear feet of 1 x 8 pine
- 55 linear feet of 2 x 4 pine
- 2 sheets (4' x 8') of ¼" plywood
- ½ sheet (4' x 4') of ½" plywood
- 1 piece of ¾" plywood, 24¾" x 72"

Hardware

- 46   ¾" wire brads
- 104   1½" (3d) finish nails
- 33   1½" (4d) finish nails
- 37   2½" (8d) finish nails
- 12   1" wood screws
- 16   1½" wood screws
- 6   2" wood screws
- 16   2½" wood screws
- 4   21-inch-long drawer glides
- 2 cabinet hinges
- 3 drawer pulls
- 1 magnetic catch

Special Tools and Techniques

- Chisel
- Long pipe clamps
- Router with ½" rabbet cutter
- Miters
- Rabbets
- Dadoes

Cutting List

Code	Description	Qty	Materials	Dimensions
A	Short Frame	8	2 x 4 pine	23¼" long
B	Long Frame	8	2 x 4 pine	28" long
C	Side	4	¼" plywood	24¼" x 28"
D	Back Frame	4	1 x 4 pine	23" long
E	Back	2	¼" plywood	23" x 28"
F	Drawer Support	6	2 x 4 pine, ripped	23¼" long
G	Horizontal Support	4	2 x 4 pine	20" long
H	Vertical Trim	4	1 x 4 pine	28" long
I	Horizontal Trim	4	1 x 4 pine	16½" long
J	Upper Drawer Front/Back	2	½" plywood	4½" x 15½"
K	Upper Drawer Side	2	½" plywood	4½" x 23"
L	Drawer Bottom	2	¼" plywood	14⅞" x 23⅜"
M	Lower Drawer Front/Back	2	½" plywood	10" x 15½"
N	Lower Drawer Side	2	½" plywood	10" x 23"
O	Upper Drawer Front	1	1 x 8 pine	18½" long
P	Vertical Drawer Frame	2	1 x 4 pine	13" long
Q	Horizontal Drawer Frame	2	1 x 4 pine	11½" long
R	Center Drawer Front	1	¼" plywood	7" x 12½"
S	Vertical Door Frame	2	1 x 4 pine	25" long
T	Horizontal Door Frame	2	1 x 4 pine	11½" long
U	Center Door Front	1	¼" plywood	12½" x 19"
V	Long Top Trim	2	1 x 4 pine	79" long
W	Short Top Trim	2	1 x 4 pine	31¾" long
X	Desk Top	1	¾" plywood	24¾" x 72"

BUILDING THE DESK BASES

1. Cut eight short frames (A) from 2 x 4 pine, each measuring 23¼ inches long.

2. Miter the ends of each of the eight short frames at opposing 45-degree angles, as shown in figure 1.

3. Cut eight long frames (B) from 2 x 4 pine, each measuring 28 inches long.

4. Miter the ends of each of the eight long frames (B) at opposing 45-degree angles, as shown in figure 1.

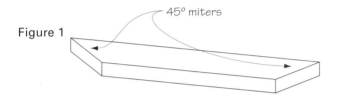

45° miters

Figure 1

5. Cut four sides (C) from ¼-inch plywood, each measuring 24¼ x 28 inches.

6. Place two long frames (B) on a level surface, parallel to each other and 21 inches apart, as shown in figure 2. Place two short frames (A) between the ends of the long frames (B), matching miters, to form a 23¼ x 28 inch rectangle. Apply glue to the meeting surfaces, and nail one side (C) over the four frames (A and B), as shown in figure 3. Note that one 28-inch edge of the side (C) extends 1 inch past the frame assembly. Use 1¼-inch (3d) finish nails spaced every 4 inches.

Figure 2

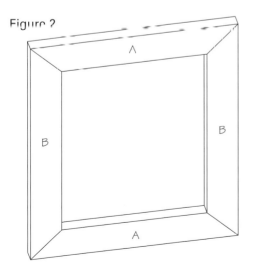

Figure 3

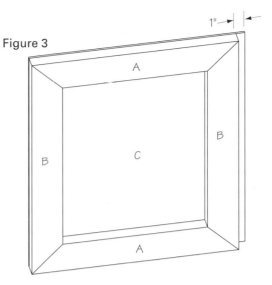

1"

7. Repeat step 6 three more times to assemble three additional frame assemblies, using the remaining six short frames (A), six long frames (B), and three sides (C).

8. Cut four back frames (D) from 1 x 4 pine, each measuring 23 inches long.

9. Place two frame assemblies on a level surface, parallel to each other, and 21½ inches apart. The 1-inch-wide side extensions should be placed on top and to the outside. Fit two back frames (D) between the two sides (C) over the long frames (B), as shown in figure 4. Apply glue to the meeting surfaces, and screw through the back frames (D) into the edges of the long frames (B). Use two 1½-inch screws on each joint.

Figure 4

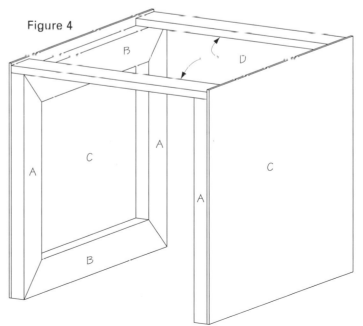

10. Repeat step 9 to attach the remaining two back frames (D) to the remaining two frame assemblies.

11. Cut two backs (E) from ¼-inch plywood, each measuring 23 x 28 inches.

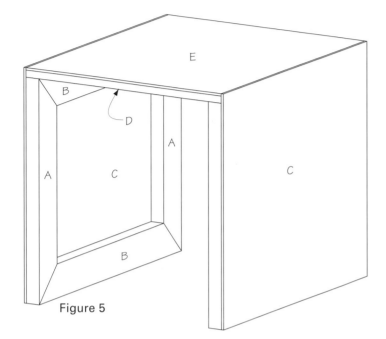

Figure 5

12. Apply glue to the meeting surfaces, and place one back (E) over the two back frames (D), as shown in figure 5. Nail through the back (E) into both back frames (D). Use five evenly spaced ¾-inch brads on each edge of each back frame (D).

13. Repeat step 12 to attach the remaining back (E) to the remaining base assembly.

COMPLETING THE DRAWER BASE ASSEMBLY

As the photograph shows, the desk has two bases. The left base consists of two drawers, and the right base has just one hinged cabinet door. This section covers the completion of the left drawer base assembly. However, some of the pieces used in the drawer base are also used in the cabinet base. Remaining pieces cut but not used in this section should be labeled and set aside for use in completing the cabinet base.

14. Rip a total of 12 linear feet of 2 x 4 pine to a width of 1¾ inches.

15. Cut six drawer supports (F) from the ripped 2 x 4 pine, each measuring 23¼ inches long.

16. Apply glue to the meeting surfaces, and attach one drawer support (F) to the left side of one base assembly, 8 inches from the top of the base assembly, as shown in figure 6. Make sure that the 1¾-inch dimension is horizontal. Screw through the drawer support (F) into the two long frames (B). Use two 2½-inch screws on each joint.

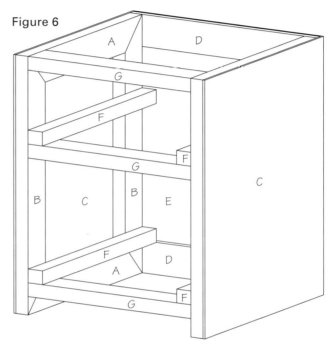

Figure 6

17. Repeat step 16 to install the second drawer support (F) opposite the first, on the right side of the base assembly.

18. Repeat steps 15 and 16 to attach the remaining two drawer supports (F) 3½ inches from the bottom of the base assembly.

19. Install the purchased drawer glides on the inside edges of each of the drawer supports (F), following the manufacturer's directions. The drawer glides we purchased took up ½ inch of horizontal space on each side. If your glides are not the same measurement, you will need to alter the horizontal dimensions of the drawer to accommodate the difference.

20. Cut four horizontal supports (G) from 2 x 4 pine, each measuring 20 inches long.

21. Attach one horizontal support (G) at the top front of the base assembly between the two support frames, as shown in figure 6. Nail through the sides (C) into the end of the horizontal support (G), using two 2½-inch (8d) finish nails on each joint.

22. Repeat step 21 two times to attach a second horizontal support (G) just below the upper two drawer supports (F), and a third horizontal support (G) just below the lower drawer supports (F).

23. Cut four vertical trims (H) from 1 x 4 pine, each measuring 28 inches long.

24. Apply glue to the meeting surfaces, and attach one vertical trim (H) to the left front of the base assembly, as shown in figure 7. Nail through the vertical trim (H) into the horizontal supports (G) and the frame support, using 1½-inch (4d) finish nails spaced every 5 inches.

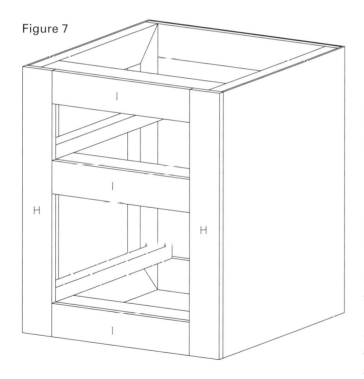

Figure 7

25. Repeat step 6 to attach a second vertical trim (H) on the right front of the base assembly.

26. Cut four horizontal trims (I) from 1 x 4 pine, each measuring 16½ inches long.

27. Attach one horizontal trim (I) at the top front of the base assembly between the two vertical trims (H), as shown in figure 7. Apply glue to the meeting surfaces, and nail through the horizontal trim (I) into the horizontal supports (G), using three evenly spaced 1½-inch (4d) finish nails.

28. Repeat step 27 to attach two more horizontal trims (I) between the two vertical trims (H) flush with the tops of the remaining horizontal supports (G), as shown in figure 7.

MAKING THE UPPER DRAWER

There are two drawers in this desk. Both are constructed as shown in the assembly diagram in figure 8. The only difference is the size of the drawer pieces.

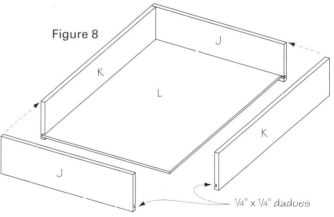

Figure 8

¼" x ¼" dadoes

29. Cut two upper drawer front/back pieces (J) from ½-inch plywood, each measuring 4½ x 15½ inches.

30. Cut two upper drawer sides (K) from ½-inch plywood, each measuring 4½ x 23 inches.

31. Cut a ¼ x ¼-inch dado on the inside of each upper drawer piece (J and K) ⅜ inch from the lower edge, to accommodate the plywood bottom.

32. Cut two drawer bottoms (L) from ¼-inch plywood, each measuring 14⅞ x 23⅞ inches.

33. Assemble the upper drawer as shown in figure 8. Note that the upper drawer front/back pieces (J) overlap the ends of the upper drawer sides (K). Use three 1½-inch (4d) finishing nails on each end of the overlapping boards. The drawer front will be added later.

34. Cut two lower drawer front/back pieces (M) from ½-inch plywood, each measuring 10 x 15½ inches.

35. Cut two lower drawer sides (N) from ½-inch plywood, each measuring 10 x 23 inches.

36. Cut a ¼ x ¼-inch dado on the inside of each lower drawer piece (M and N) ⅜ inch from the lower edge, to accommodate the plywood bottom.

37. Repeat the drawer assembly in step 33 using the remaining drawer bottom (L), the lower drawer fronts (M), and the lower drawer sides (N).

38. Attach the upper and lower drawers to the drawer glides, following the manufacturer's instructions.

MAKING THE DRAWER FRONTS

39. Cut one upper drawer front (O) from 1 x 8 pine, measuring 18½ inches long.

40. The lower drawer front consists of ¼-inch plywood framed with 1 x 4 pine. Cut two vertical drawer frames (P) from 1 x 4 pine, each measuring 13 inches long.

41. Cut two horizontal drawer frames (Q) from 1 x 4 pine, each measuring 11½ inches long.

42. Place the two vertical drawer frames (P) on a level surface, parallel to each other and 11½ inches apart. Fit the two horizontal drawer frames (Q) between the ends of the two vertical drawer frames, as shown in figure 9. Apply glue to the meeting surfaces, and clamp the assembly for a few hours.

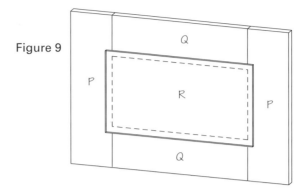

Figure 9

43. To temporarily reinforce the joints for the next step, use a staple gun to staple three times over each joint. Then rout the inside edges of the assembled drawer front frame, ¼ inch deep and ½ inch wide. Square the corners with a chisel. Remove the staples.

44. Cut one center drawer front (R) from ¼-inch plywood, measuring 7 x 12½ inches.

45. Apply glue to the meeting surfaces, and fit the center drawer front (R) into the routed edges of the assembled drawer front frame. Nail through the center drawer front (R) into the routed edges of the vertical drawer frames (P) and the horizontal drawer frames (Q). Use ¾-inch brads driven at an angle and spaced every 4 inches.

46. To attach the drawer fronts to the assembled drawers, place a piece of wood between the back of each drawer and the back of the desk assembly so that the drawers are held flush with the front of the desk. Use heavy-duty double-sided tape to hold both drawer fronts in place temporarily until you have both drawer fronts positioned exactly right. The drawer fronts should be centered over the openings in the front of the drawer base. Then attach the fronts to the drawers. Use 1-inch screws to screw through the drawer into the drawer front on the upper drawer and into the drawer frame on the lower drawer. Use four screws on the upper drawer and eight screws on the lower one.

COMPLETING THE CABINET DOOR BASE ASSEMBLY

47. Attach the remaining horizontal support (G) at the top front of the remaining base assembly between the two support frames, as shown in figure 6. Nail through the sides (C) into the end of the horizontal support (G), using two 2½-inch nails on each joint.

48. Apply glue to the meeting surfaces, and attach one drawer support (F) to the left side of the base assembly, flush with the bottom of the base assembly. Screw through the drawer support (F) into the two long frames (B) and the lower short frame (A). Use five 2½-inch screws evenly spaced.

49. Repeat step 48 to attach the remaining lower drawer support (F) to the opposite side of the base assembly.

50. Apply glue to the meeting surfaces, and attach one vertical trim (H) to the left front of the base assembly, as shown in figure 7. Nail through the vertical trim (H) into the horizontal support (G), the frame support, and the drawer support (F). Use 1½-inch (4d) finish nails spaced every 5 inches.

51. Repeat step 50 to attach the remaining vertical trim (H) on the right front of the base assembly.

52. Attach the remaining horizontal trim (I) to the top front of the base assembly between the two vertical trims (H), as shown in figure 7. Apply glue to the meeting surfaces, and nail through the horizontal trim (I) into the horizontal support (G). Use three evenly spaced 1½-inch (4d) finish nails.

MAKING THE DOOR

53. The door consists of ¼-inch plywood framed with 1 x 4 pine. Cut two vertical door frames (S) from 1 x 4 pine, each measuring 25 inches long.

54. Cut two horizontal door frames (T) from 1 x 4 pine, each measuring 11½ inches long.

55. Place the two vertical door frames (S) on a level surface, parallel to each other and 11½ inches apart. Fit the two horizontal door frames (T) between the ends of the two vertical door frames, as shown in figure 9. Apply glue to the meeting surfaces and clamp the assembly overnight.

56. To temporarily reinforce the joints for the next step, use a staple gun to staple three times over each joint. Then rout the inside edges of the assembled door front frame, ¼ inch deep and ½ inch wide. Use a chisel to square the corners and remove the staples.

57. Cut one center door front (U) from ¼-inch plywood, measuring 12½ x 19 inches.

58. Apply glue to the meeting surfaces, and fit the center door front (U) into the routed edges of the assembled door front frame. Nail through the center door front (U) into the routed edges of the vertical door frames (S) and the horizontal door frames (T). Use ¾-inch brads driven at an angle and spaced every four inches.

59. Attach the door to the base assembly using two cabinet hinges. The door should be hung ¼ inch from the bottom of the base assembly and centered horizontally.

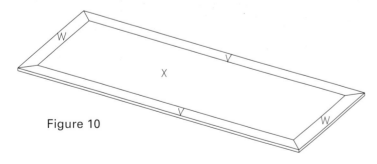

Figure 10

MAKING THE DESKTOP

60. Cut two long top trims (V) from 1 x 4 pine, each measuring 79 inches long.

61. Miter both ends of each long top trim (V) at opposing 45-degree angles, as shown in figure 1.

62. Cut two short top trims (W) from 1 x 4 pine, each measuring 31¾ inches long.

63. Miter both ends of each short top trim (W) at opposing 45-degree angles, as shown in figure 1.

64. Cut one desk top (X) from ¾-inch plywood, measuring 24¾ x 72 inches.

65. Place the desk top (X) on a level surface. Position the long and short top trims (V and W) along the outer edges of the desk top (X), as shown in figure 10. Apply glue to the meeting edges, and clamp the five pieces of wood together with pipe clamps for a few hours. The result is a desktop that now measures 31¾ x 79 inches.

66. Place the two base assemblies on a level surface, parallel to each other and 24½ inches apart. Center the desktop over the two base assemblies. Attach the three pieces together by screwing through the top horizontal supports (G) into the desktop. Use three 2-inch screws on each joint. Do not use glue, as you would be unable to disassemble the desk for moving.

FINISHING

67. Fill any screw holes or imperfections in the wood with wood filler.

68. Thoroughly sand all of the wood parts on the completed desk.

69. Stain or paint the desk the color of your choice. We chose a whitewash stain for our desk.

70. Install the three drawer pulls on the two drawers and the door. Also install a magnetic catch on the door.

Pine Bed

This great-looking pine bed is similar to one that we found in a furniture store. The big difference is the price. We made the headboard and footboard of ordinary pine and then attached them to a standard metal bedframe. We are proud of the result and even more proud of the money we saved.

pine bed

Materials

The materials specified are for a queen-size headboard and footboard. If your bed is larger or smaller, the materials must be adjusted accordingly. See the Cutting List Note specifying sizes adjusted for twin- and king-size beds.

- 75 linear feet of 1 x 4 pine
- 20 linear feet of 2 x 4 pine
- 2 linear feet of 2 x 6 pine

Hardware

- 110 1¼" (3d) finish nails
- 100 1½" (4d) finish nails
- 16   2½" (8d) finish nails
- 16   2" screws

Special Tools and Techniques

- Pipe clamps
- Dadoes

Cutting List

Code	Description	Qty.	Materials	Dimensions
A	Headboard Top/Bottom	2	2 x 4 pine	56" long
B	Headboard Slat	16	1 x 4 pine	10" long
C	Headboard Post Vertical	8	1 x 4 pine	41½" long
D	Headboard Post Cap	2	2 x 6 pine	5½" long
E	Footboard Top/Bottom	2	2 x 4 pine	56" long
F	Footboard Slat	16	1 x 4 pine	8½" long
G	Footboard Post Vertical	8	1 x 4 pine	25½" long
H	Footboard Post Cap	2	2 x 6 pine	5½" long

✳ Cutting List Notes

For a twin-size bed, the headboard top/bottoms (A) and the footboard top/bottoms (E) should be 35 inches long, and you will need 10 headboard slats (B) and 10 footboard slats (F). Instead of the materials listed, you will need only 65 linear feet of 1 x 4 pine and 14 linear feet of 2 x 4 pine.

For a king-size bed, the headboard top/bottoms (A) and the footboard top/bottoms (E) should be 73½ inches long, and you will need 21 headboard slats (B) and 21 footboard slats (F). Therefore, you will need 84 linear feet of 1 x 4 pine and 26 linear feet of 2 x 4 pine.

MAKING THE HEADBOARD

1. Cut two headboard top/bottoms (A) from 2 x 4 pine, each measuring 56 inches long.

2. Cut a ¾-inch-wide dado, ½ inch deep, down the length of one edge of each of the headboard top/bottoms (A), as shown in figure 1.

3. Cut sixteen headboard slats (B) from 1 x 4 pine, each measuring 10 inches long.

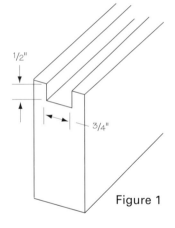

Figure 1

4. Working on a level surface, place the two headboard top/bottoms (A) parallel to each other, with the dadoes to the inside, as shown in figure 2. Fit the ends of the sixteen headboard slats (B) into the dadoes in the headboard top/bottoms (A). When the headboard slats are properly fitted, the distance between the two headboard top/bottoms should measure 9 inches. When the positions are perfect, the overall measurement of the headboard assembly should be 16 inches high and 56 inches long. Secure the slats by nailing through the back of the dadoed edge of the headboard top/bottoms (A) into the ends of the headboard slats (B), using two 1¼-inch (3d) finish nails on each joint.

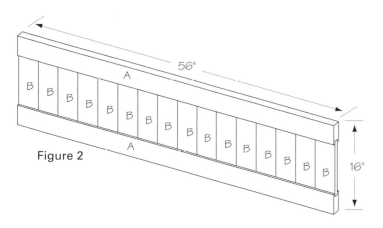

56"

A

B B B B B B B B B B B B B B B B

A

16"

Figure 2

ADDING THE HEADBOARD POSTS

5. Cut eight headboard post verticals (C) from 1 x 4 pine, each measuring 41½ inches long.

6. In order to center the completed headboard posts, the first headboard post vertical (C) must be offset when it is attached to the headboard assembly. Refer to figure 3 to mark the placement of the headboard assembly on the first headboard post vertical (C).

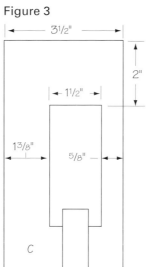

Figure 3

3½"

2"

1½"

1³⁄₈"

5⁄₈"

C

7. Repeat step 6 to mark a mirror-image placement on a second headboard post vertical (C).

0. Position the headboard assembly between the marked verticals (C), exactly on the placement marks, as shown in figure 4. Apply glue to the edges of the outer slats, and use clamps to hold the assembly together. Screw through the verticals (C) into the ends of the headboard top/bottoms (A), using two 2-inch screws on each joint.

9. Add three more verticals (C) to each of the attached verticals (C), overlapping each piece in rotation, as shown in figure 5. Secure each of the verticals (C) with glue and 1½-inch (4d) finish nails spaced every 4 inches along the length. Make certain that you follow the rotation exactly to form the first post and then reverse the rotation for the other post. Otherwise, your posts will not match.

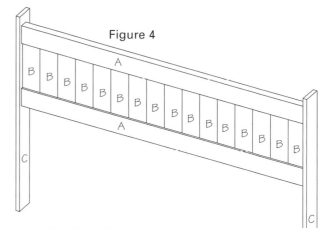

Figure 4

A

B B B B B B B B B B B B B B B B

A

C

C

10. Cut two headboard post caps (D) from 2 x 6 pine, each measuring 5½ inches long.

11. Center one headboard post cap (D) over one assembled post. Nail through the headboard post cap (D) into each of the verticals (C), using four 2½-inch (8d) finish nails.

12. Repeat step 11 to attach the remaining headboard post cap (D) to the remaining post.

MAKING THE FOOTBOARD

13. Cut two footboard top/bottoms (E) from 2 x 4 pine, each measuring 56 inches long.

14. Cut a ¾-inch-wide dado, ½-inch deep down the length of one edge of each of the footboard top/bottoms (E), as shown in figure 1.

15. Cut sixteen footboard slats (F) from 1 x 4 pine, each measuring 8½ inches long.

16. Working on a level surface, place the two footboard top/bottoms (E) parallel to each other, with the dadoes to the inside, in the same manner as shown in figure 2. Fit the ends of the sixteen footboard slats (F) into the dadoes in the footboard top/bottoms (E). When the footboard slats are properly fitted, the distance between the two footboard top/bottoms should measure 7½ inches. When the positions are perfect, the overall measurement of the footboard assembly should be 14½ inches high and 56 inches long. Secure the slats by nailing through the back of the dadoed edge of the footboard top/bottoms (E) into the ends of the footboard slats (F), using two 1¼-inch (3d) finish nails on each joint.

ADDING THE FOOTBOARD POSTS

17. Cut eight footboard post verticals (G) from 1 x 4 pine, each measuring 25½ inches long.

18. In order to center the completed footboard posts, the first footboard post vertical (G) must be offset when it is attached to the footboard assembly. Refer to figure 3 to mark the placement of the footboard assembly on the first footboard post vertical (G).

19. Repeat step 18 to mark a mirror-image placement on a second footboard post vertical (G).

20. Position the footboard assembly between the marked verticals (G), exactly on the placement marks. Apply glue to the edges of the outer slats, and use clamps to hold the assembly together. Screw through the verticals (G) into the ends of the footboard top/bottom (E) using two 2-inch screws on each joint.

21. Add three more verticals (G) to each of the attached verticals (G), overlapping each piece in rotation, as shown in figure 5. As you did for the headboard, make certain that you follow the rotation exactly to form the first post, and then reverse the rotation for the other post.

22. Cut two footboard post caps (H) from 2 x 6 pine, each measuring 5½ inches long.

23. Center one footboard post cap (H) over one assembled post. Nail through the post cap (H) into each of the verticals (G), using four 2½-inch (8d) finish nails.

24. Repeat step 23 to attach the remaining footboard post cap (H) over the remaining post.

FINISHING

25. Fill the screw holes, crevices, and cracks with wood filler.

26. Sand all surfaces of the completed headboard and footboard.

27. Stain or paint the headboard and footboard the color of your choice. We chose to retain the natural color of the pine and simply seal it with a gloss polyurethane.

28. We already had a metal frame with brackets for both a headboard and footboard, so we simply positioned the headboard and footboard and screwed through the metal brackets into the posts on both the headboard and footboard. If your frame has only one bracket, you can turn the frame around and attach that bracket to the footboard. Then you can either attach the headboard to the wall or simply place the headboard against the wall and push the bed against it to hold it in place.

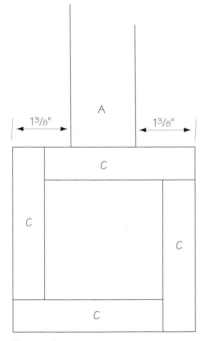

Figure 5

Nightstand

Our nightstand is a practical addition to any bedroom. The lower shelf holds books and magazines, and the drawer is large enough to store nighttime necessities.

Materials

- 22 linear feet of 1 x 4 pine
- ½ sheet of ¼" plywood (4' x 4')
- 1 sheet of ¾" plywood (4' x 8')
- 11 linear feet of ¾"-wide rope molding
- 2 linear feet of 3"-wide beaded molding

Hardware

- Approximately 4 5¾" brads
- Approximately 15 1" (2d) finish nails
- Approximately 20 1¼" (3d) finish nails
- Approximately 85 1½" (4d) finish nails
- 1 drawer pull

Special Tools and Techniques

- Bar clamps or pipe clamps
- Dadoes

Cutting List

Code	Description	Qty	Materials	Dimensions
A	Vertical Trim	4	1 x 4 pine	23" long
B	Horizontal Trim	4	1 x 4 pine	8" long
C	Sides	2	¼" plywood	15" x 23"
D	Back	1	¾" plywood	22½" x 23"
E	Shelf	2	¾" plywood	22½" x 14¼"
F	Drawer Guides	2	1 x 4 pine	14¼" long
G	Top Supports	2	1 x 4 pine	22½" long
H	Front Vertical Trim	2	1 x 4 pine	23" long
I	Bottom Trim	1	3"-wide beaded molding	17½" long
J	Shelf Trim	2	¾"-wide rope molding	17½" long
K	Top	1	¾" plywood	16 ¾" x 26½"
L	Top Trim	4	¾"-wide rope molding	cut to fit
M	Drawer Front/Back	2	¾" plywood	5⅝" x 17⅜"
N	Drawer Sides	2	¾" plywood	5⅝" x 12¾"
O	Drawer Bottom	1	¼" plywood	13 1/8" x 16¼"

BUILDING THE SIDES

1. Cut four vertical trims (A) from 1 x 4 pine, each measuring 23 inches long.

2. Cut four horizontal trims (B) from 1 x 4 pine, each measuring 8 inches long.

3. Cut two sides (C) from ¼-inch beaded plywood, each measuring 15 x 23 inches.

4. Place two vertical trims (A), better faces down, on a level surface, parallel to each other and 8 inches apart. Fit two horizontal trims (B), better faces down, between the ends of the vertical trims (A), as shown in figure 1.

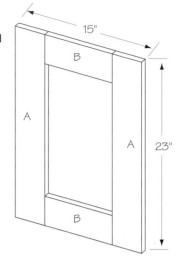

Figure 1

5. Apply glue to the faces of the trims (A and B). Place one side (C) (beaded side down) over the horizontal and vertical trims (A and B), matching all four edges. Nail through the side (C), 1 inch from each of the edges, using ¾-inch brads spaced about 4 inches apart.

6. Repeat steps 4 and 5 to assemble a second side, using the remaining two vertical trims (A), two horizontal trims (B), and side (C).

COMPLETING THE BASE ASSEMBLY

7. Cut one back (D) from ¾-inch plywood, measuring 22½ x 23 inches.

8. Place the two side assemblies on a level surface, on edge, parallel to each other and 22½ inches apart.

9. Place the back (D) between the two side assemblies, matching the 23-inch edges, as shown in figure 2. Nail through the side assemblies into the edge of the back (D), using 1½-inch (4d) nails placed every 4 inches.

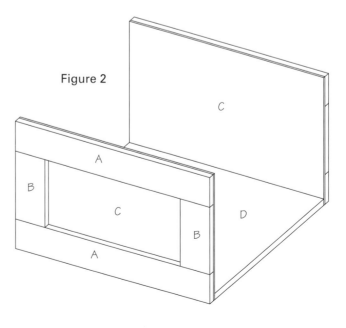

Figure 2

10. Cut two shelves (E) from ¾-inch plywood, each measuring 22½ x 14¼ inches.

11. Cut two drawer guides (F) from 1 x 4 pine, each measuring 14¼ inches long.

12. Attach both drawer guides (F) to one shelf (E), 1¾ inches from each 15-inch edge, as shown in figure 3. Nail through the shelf (E) into the edges of the drawer guides (F), using four 1½-inch (4d) nails on each joint.

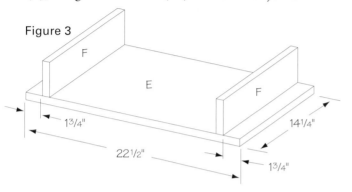

Figure 3

13. Attach the shelf (E) without the drawer guides 2¾ inches from what will be the bottom of the cabinet, as shown in figure 4. Nail through the side assemblies into the edges, using four 1½-inch (4d) nails on each joint.

14. Repeat step 13 to attach the remaining shelf (E), with the drawer guides facing the top of the cabinet, 6½ inches from the top of the cabinet, as shown in figure 4.

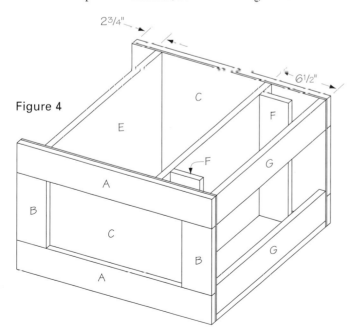

Figure 4

15. Cut two top supports (G) from 1 x 4 pine, each measuring 22½ inches long.

16. Attach one top support (G) between the two side assemblies, flush with the top edge of the back (D), as shown in figure 4. Nail through the side assemblies into the ends of the top support, using two 1½-inch (4d) nails on each joint.

17. Repeat step 16 to attach the remaining top support (G) between the two side assemblies, flush with the front and top of the base assembly, as shown in figure 4.

ADDING THE TRIM

18. Cut two front vertical trims (H) from 1 x 4 pine, each measuring 23 inches long.

19. Apply glue to the meeting surfaces, and attach one front vertical trim (H) to the edge of the left side assembly, as shown in figure 5. Nail through the front vertical trim (H) into the side assembly, the two shelves (E), the drawer guide (F), and the top support (G). Use 1½-inch (4d) nails spaced every 4 inches.

20. Repeat step 19 to attach the remaining vertical trim (H) to the edge of the right side assembly, as shown in figure 5.

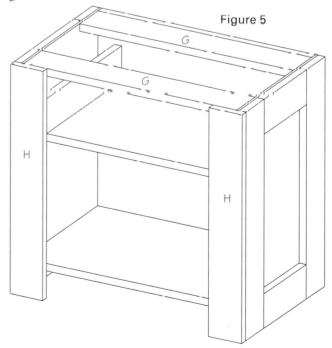

Figure 5

21. Cut one bottom trim (I) from 3-inch-wide beaded molding, measuring 17½ inches long.

22. Apply glue to the meeting surfaces, and nail the bottom trim (I) between the two vertical trims (H), flush with the top of the lower shelf (E). Use 1-inch (2d) nails spaced about every 4 inches.

23. Cut two shelf trims (J) from ¾-inch-wide rope molding, each measuring 17½ inches long.

24. Apply glue to the meeting surfaces, and nail one shelf trim over the exposed edge of the top support (G), between the two vertical trims (H). Use 1-inch (2d) nails spaced about every 4 inches.

25. Nail the remaining shelf trim (J) over the exposed edge of the upper shelf (E), between the vertical trims (H). Use 1-inch (2d) nails spaced about every 4 inches.

CONSTRUCTING THE TOP

26. Cut one top (K) from ¾-inch plywood, measuring 16¾ x 26½ inches.

27. Cut and fit four top trims (L) from ¾-inch-wide rope molding to fit over the four exposed edges of the top (K), mitering the top trims (L) at each of the corners. Use glue and 1½-inch (4d) nails spaced every 4 inches to attach the top trims (L) to the top (K).

28. Place the base assembly upright and place the top assembly over it. The top assembly should be centered widthwise, with the edge of the plywood top (K) flush with the back of the cabinet, and overhanging the front. When the position is correct, apply glue on the meeting surfaces, and nail through the top assembly into the top supports (G), using six 1¼-inch (3d) nails.

MAKING THE DRAWER

29. Cut two drawer front/backs (M) from ¾-inch plywood, each measuring 5⅝ x 17⅜ inches.

30. Cut two drawer sides (N) from ¾-inch plywood, each measuring 5⅝ x 12¾ inches.

31. Cut one drawer bottom (O) from ¼-inch plywood, measuring 13⅛ x 16¼ inches.

32. Cut a ¼ x ¼-inch dado on the inside of each drawer piece (M and N) ⅜ inch from the lower edge, to accommodate the drawer bottom (O).

33. Assemble the drawer as shown in figure 6. Note that the drawer front/back pieces (M) overlap the ends of the drawer sides (N). Use two 1½-inch (4d) nails on each end of the overlapping boards.

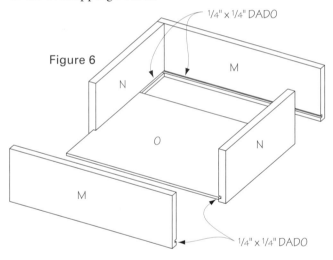

Figure 6

¼" x ¼" DADO

¼" x ¼" DADO

FINISHING

34. Fill any nail holes or imperfections in the wood with wood filler.

35. Thoroughly sand all of the wood parts on the completed night stand.

36. Stain or paint the nightstand the color of your choice. We chose to retain the natural wood color and simply sealed it with polyurethane.

37. Install the drawer pull in the center of the nightstand drawer.

Armoire

This attractive and practical two-door armoire takes up very little floor space in the bedroom but provides lots of storage. Because it is only a little over a foot deep, it's easy to incorporate into almost any room, yet it conveniently keeps socks, sweaters, ties, and belts organized and handy.

armoire

Materials

- 6 linear feet of 1 x 1 pine
- 40 linear feet of 1 x 4 pine
- 28 linear feet of 1 x 6 pine
- 38 linear feet of 1 x 12 pine
- 16 linear feet of 3" crown molding
- 2 sheets (4' x 8') of ¼" plywood
- 4 porch post finials, 7½" tall*
- 2 linear feet of wooden closet rod (optional)

Hardware

- 110 ¾" wire brads
- 52 1¼" (3d) finish nails
- 40 2" (6d) finish nails
- 44 1" wood screws
- 110 1½" wood screws
- 6 cabinet door hinges
- 2 door pulls
- 2 cabinet catches

Special Tools and Techniques

- Bar clamps or pipe clamps
- Miters
- Rabbets

Cutting List

Code	Description	Qty	Materials	Dimensions
A	Top/Bottom	2	1 x 12 pine	42¼" long
B	Side	2	1 x 12 pine	61¼" long
C	Center Divider	1	1 x 12 pine	61¼" long
D	Shelf	8	1 x 12 pine	20" long
E	Shelf Support	6	1 x 1 pine	11¼" long
F	Back	1	¼" plywood	42¼" x 62¾"
G	Side Trim	4	1 x 4 pine	11¼" long
H	Front Trim	2	1 x 4 pine	43¾" long
I	Crown Molding	6	3" crown molding	cut to fit
J	Drawer Front/Back	10	1 x 6 pine	19⅞" long
K	Drawer Side	10	1 x 6 pine	9⅝" long
L	Drawer Bottom	4	¼" plywood	10" x 18¾"
M	Top/Bottom Door Trim	4	1 x 4 pine	21" long
N	Side Door Trim	4	1 x 4 pine	61" long
O	Door Panel	2	¼" plywood	14½" x 54½"
P	Leg	4	porch post finials*	7½" long

*Notes on Materials

The legs for our armoire are actually porch post finials which we purchased in a building supply store. The exact shape doesn't matter, but they should be at least 7½ inches long. If you can't find the exact finials that we used, you can lengthen smaller finials by attaching a 2 x 4 block under the lower trim on the armoire and then attaching the finials to those blocks.

BUILDING THE ARMOIRE OUTER CASE

1. Cut two top/bottoms (A) from 1 x 12 pine, each measuring 42¼ inches.

2. Cut two sides (B) from 1 x 12 pine, each measuring 61¼ inches long.

3. Place the two sides (B) on edge on a level surface, parallel to each other and 40¾ inches apart. Place the two top/bottoms (A) over the ends of the two sides (B), as shown in figure 1. Screw through the top/bottoms (A) into the two sides (B), using four evenly spaced 1½-inch screws on each joint.

4. Cut one center divider (C) from 1 x 2 pine, measuring 61¼ inches long.

5. Place the center divider (C) in the center of the armoire assembly, parallel to and 20 inches from each of the sides (B), as shown in figure 1. Screw through the top/bottoms (A) into the center divider (C), using four evenly spaced 1½-inch screws on each joint.

6. Cut eight shelves (D) from 1 x 12 pine, each measuring 20 inches long.

7. Refer to figure 2 to place five shelves (D) on the right side of the armoire case. Note that the upper shelf (D) is 28¾ inches below the top/bottom (A) and that the remaining four shelves (D) are spaced 5¾ inches apart. Screw through the side (B) and center divider (C) into the five shelves (D). Use four evenly spaced 1½-inch screws on each joint.

8. Refer to figure 2 to place the three remaining shelves (D) on the left side of the armoire case. Note that the upper shelf (D) is 14¾ inches below the top/bottom (A) and that the remaining two shelves are spaced 14¾ inches apart. Screw through the side (B) and center divider (C) into the three shelves (D). Use four evenly spaced 1½-inch screws on each joint.

9. Cut six left shelf supports (E) from 1 x 1 pine, each measuring 11¼ inches long.

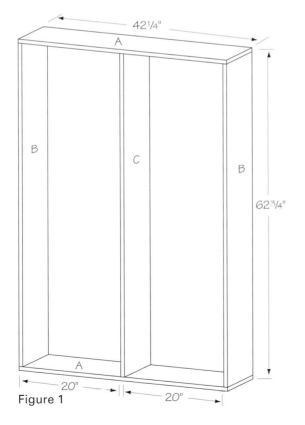

Figure 1

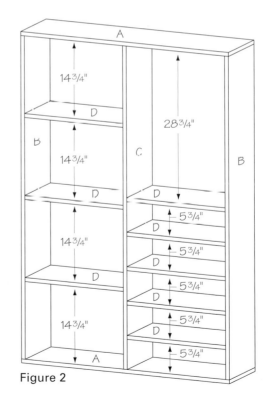

Figure 2

10. Glue and nail one shelf support (E) under the left side of the upper shelf (D), as shown in figure 3. Apply glue to the meeting surfaces, and nail through the shelf support (E) into the shelf (D) and the side (B), using three 1¼-inch (3d) nails in each direction.

11. Repeat step 10 five more times to install a shelf support (E) under each side of each left shelf (D), as shown in figure 3.

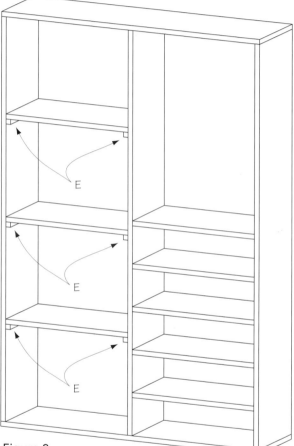

Figure 3

12. Cut one back (F) from ¼-inch plywood, measuring 42¼ x 62¾ inches.

13. With the armoire case lying on its front, apply glue to the back edges of the top/bottoms (A), sides (B), center divider (C), and shelves (D). With the help of a friend, lay the back (F) on the armoire case, matching all outside edges. Screw through the back (F) into the edges of the top/bottoms (A), sides (B), and center divider (C), using 1-inch screws spaced 6 inches apart.

ADDING THE TRIM

14. Cut four side trims (G) from 1 x 4 pine, each measuring 11¼ inches long.

15. Place the armoire case on its back on a level surface. Screw one side trim (G) to the top of the armoire case, covering only the edge of the top/bottom (A), as shown in figure 4. Screw through the side trim (G) into the top/bottom (A), using four evenly spaced 1½-inch screws.

16. Repeat step 2 three more times to attach the remaining three side trims (G) to the top/bottoms (A) on the bottom and top of the armoire case.

17. Cut two front trims (H) from 1 x 4 pine, each measuring 43¾ inches long.

18. Apply glue to the meeting surfaces and screw one front trim (H) to the top front of the armoire case over the ends of the two side trims (G), as shown in figure 4. Screw through the front trim (H) into the side trims (G) and the edge of the top/bottom (A), using 1½-inch screws spaced every 5 inches.

Figure 4

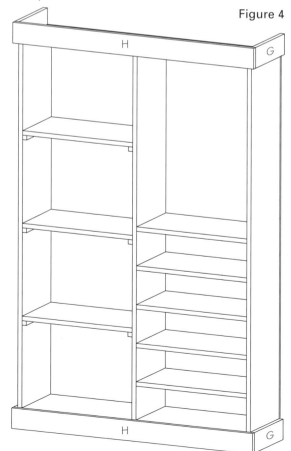

19. Repeat step 18 to attach the remaining front trim (H) to the bottom front of the armoire case.

20. The photograph shows the position of the crown molding (I) at the top and bottom of the armoire. Measure carefully and cut lengths of 3-inch-wide crown molding (I) to fit over the front and side trims (G and H) on both the bottom and top of the armoire case. The crown molding (I) should barely overlap the top trims (G and H) by ½ inch. The lower crown molding covers all but 1 inch of the bottom trims (G and H). Apply glue to the meeting surfaces, and use ¾-inch brads spaced about every 4 inches. If you are inexperienced at cutting crown molding, please refer to the "Tools, Techniques, and Materials" section at the beginning of this book.

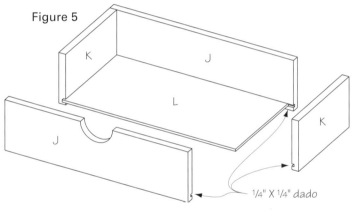

Figure 5

1/4" X 1/4" dado

MAKING THE DRAWERS

There are five identical drawers in this armoire. All five are constructed as shown in the assembly diagram in figure 5.

21. Cut ten drawer front/backs (J) from 1 x 6 pine, each measuring 19⅞ inches long.

22. Cut a half-circle with a radius of 1¾ inches from the center of five of the front/back pieces. These now will be designated the drawer fronts.

23. Cut ten drawer sides (K) from 1 x 6 pine, each measuring 9⅝ inches long.

24. Cut five drawer bottoms (L) from ¼-inch plywood, measuring 10 x 18¾ inches.

25. Cut a ¼ x ¼-inch dado on the inside of each drawer piece (J and K) ⅜ inch from the lower edge to accommodate the plywood bottom.

26. Assemble one drawer as shown in figure 5. Note that the drawer front/back pieces (J) overlap the ends of the drawer sides (K). Use two 2-inch (6d) finish nails through each end of the overlapping drawer front/backs (J).

27. Repeat the drawer assembly four more times using the remaining eight drawer front/back pieces (J), the eight drawer sides (K), and the four drawer bottoms (L).

MAKING THE DOORS

28. Cut four top/bottom door trims (M) from 1 x 4 pine, each measuring 21 inches long.

29. Miter each of the four top/bottom door trims (M) at opposing 45-degree angles, as shown in figure 6.

30. Cut four side door trims (N) from 1 x 4 pine, each measuring 61 inches long.

31. Miter each of the four side door trims (N) at opposing 45-degree angles, as shown in figure 6.

32. Cut a ¼ x ¼-inch rabbet on the inside edges of the backs of the door trims (M and N), as shown in figure 6.

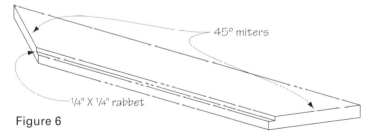

45° miters

1/4" X 1/4" rabbet

Figure 6

33. Cut two door panels (O) from ¼-inch plywood, each measuring 14½ x 54½ inches.

34. Place two top/bottom door trims (M), fronts down, 54 inches apart, and parallel to each other. The miters should oppose each other, as shown in figure 7.

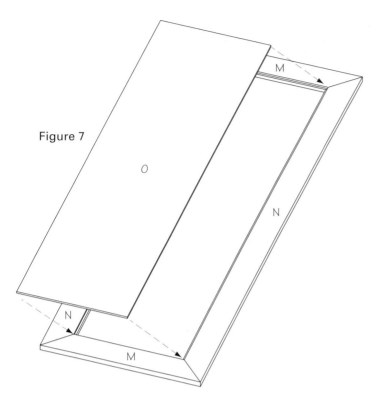

Figure 7

35. Fit two side door trims (N) between the two top/bottom door trims (M), as shown in figure 7. Apply glue to the mitered surfaces and to the rabbets. Lay one door panel into the rabbet and clamp the door assembly together. Nail through the door panel (O) at an angle into the door trims (M and N), using ¾-inch brads spaced 4 inches apart. Reinforce the outside of each miter joint by driving one 1¼-inch (3d) finish nail across the joint from each edge, starting about 1 inch from the corner.

36. Repeat steps 34 and 35 using the remaining two top/bottom door trims (M), two side door trims (N), and door panel (O).

FINISHING

37. Install the legs (P) in the four corners of the bottom of the armoire. Use three 3-inch screws driven through the bottom (A) into the top of each leg (P).

38. Fill the screw holes, crevices, and cracks with wood filler.

39. Sand all surfaces of the completed armoire.

40. Install the cabinet doors on the completed armoire using three hinges on each door.

41. Install the closet rod (optional) on the right side of the armoire.

42. Stain or paint the armoire the color of your choice. We chose to paint our armoire a bright white and then seal it with polyurethane.

43. Install the door pulls and catches.

Bathroom Cabinet

This timeless bathroom cabinet is at home with any decor! Whether your tastes are traditional or modern, this handy storage unit will fit right in. Use it to store extra towels, cologne and perfumes, and other bathroom necessaries.

bathroom cabinet

Materials

- 18 linear feet of 1 x 2 pine
- 4 linear feet of 1 x 8 pine
- 4 linear feet of 1 x 10 pine
- 2 pieces of double-strength glass (⅛" thick), each 5⅞" x 19⅜"
- 1 piece of double-strength glass (⅛" thick), 15¼" x 19¼"
- 1 piece of ½-inch plywood, 18" x 22"

Hardware

- 36 1½" (4d) finish nails
- 10 1½" screws
- 12 corrugated fasteners (or 24 1½" (4d) finish nails)
- 1 cabinet pull
- 2 cabinet hinges
- 1 door catch

Special Tools and Techniques

- Bar clamps
- Miters
- Dadoes

Cutting List

Code	Description	Qty	Materials	Dimensions
A	Vertical Side	4	1 x 2 pine	22" long
B	Horizontal Side	4	1 x 2 pine	8½" long
C	Side Glass	2	double-strength glass	5⅞" x 19⅜"
D	Back	1	½-inch plywood	22" x 18"
E	Shelf	2	1 x 8 pine	18" long
F	Top/Bottom	2	1 x 10 pine	22" long
G	Door Side	2	1 x 2 pine	21⅞" long
H	Door Top/Bottom	2	1 x 2 pine	17⅞" long
I	Door Glass	1	double-strength glass	15¼" x 19¼"

BUILDING THE CABINET SIDES

1. Each of the two sides of the cabinet and the door is a 1 x 2 frame that has been slotted in the center to accommodate a piece of glass. Dado a total of 18 linear feet of 1 x 2 pine down the center of one edge the width of a saw kerf (about ⅛ inch) and ¼ inch deep, as shown in figure 1. This may be done with a circular saw with a ripping fence, a table saw, or a router with a ⅛-inch straight cutter.

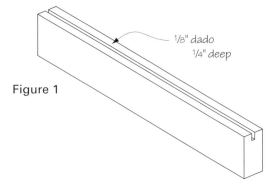

⅛" dado
¼" deep

Figure 1

2. Cut four vertical sides (A) from the dadoed 1 x 2 pine, each measuring 22 inches long.

3. Miter each end of the four vertical sides (A) at opposing 45-degree angles, as shown in figure 2. Make certain that the dadoed edge is on the short side of each piece.

4. Cut four horizontal sides (B) from the dadoed 1 x 2 pine, each measuring 8½ inches long.

5. Miter each end of the four horizontal sides (B) at opposing 45-degree angles, as shown in figure 2. Again, make certain that the dadoed edge is on the short side of each piece.

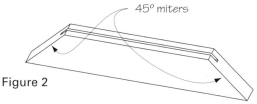

45° miters

Figure 2

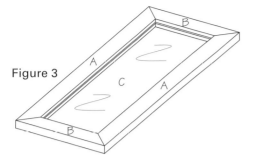

Figure 3

6. Place two vertical sides (A) on a level surface, parallel to each other and 5½ inches apart, as shown in figure 3. Fit two horizontal sides (B) between the ends of the vertical sides (A), matching miters. Fit one side glass (C) into the dadoes cut in all four sides. Make certain that the assembly is square. Apply glue to the miters, and use corrugated fasteners across each of the corner joints to secure them. You may choose to clamp these pieces together while you drive 1½-inch (4d) finish nails into the edge near each corner and across the miter joint. Use two opposing nails on each joint.

7. Repeat step 6 to assemble a second cabinet side.

COMPLETING THE CABINET

8. Cut one back (D) from ½-inch plywood, measuring 22 x 18 inches.

9. Place the two assembled sides on edge on a level surface, parallel to each other and 18 inches apart. Place the back (D) between the two sides, matching the 22-inch-long edges, as shown in figure 4. Screw through the vertical sides (A) into the edges of the back (D), using five 1½-inch screws on each joint.

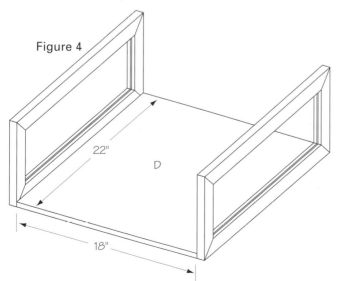

Figure 4

22"

D

18"

10. Cut two shelves (E) from 1 x 8 pine, each measuring 18 inches long.

11. Fit one shelf (E) between the two side assemblies, 6 inches from the bottom of the cabinet, and flush against the back (D), as shown in figure 5. Nail through the cabinet vertical sides (A) into the shelf (E), using two 1½-inch (4d) finish nails on each joint.

12. Repeat step 4 to attach the second shelf (E) 6 inches above the first, as shown in figure 5.

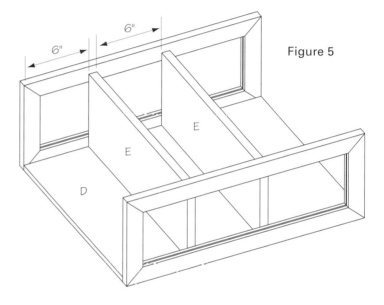

6"   6"

E

E

D

Figure 5

13. Cut two top/bottoms (F) from 1 x 10 pine, each measuring 22 inches long.

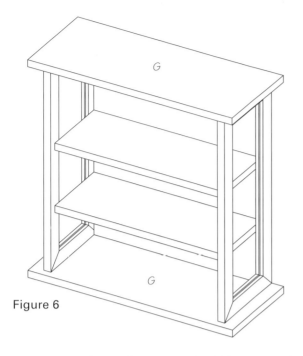

Figure 6

19. Miter each end of both door top/bottoms (H) at opposing 45-degree angles, as shown in figure 2. Again, make certain that the dadoed edge is on the narrow side of each piece.

20. Place the two door sides (G) on a level surface, parallel to each other and 14⅞ inches apart, in the same manner as shown in figure 3. Fit two door top/bottoms (H) between the ends of the door sides (G), matching miters. Fit one door glass (I) into the dadoes cut in all four pieces. Make certain that the assembly is square, apply glue to the miters, and use corrugated fasteners across each of the corner joints to secure them. You may choose to clamp these pieces together while you drive 1½-inch (4d) finish nails into the edge near each corner and across the miter joint. Use two opposing nails on each joint.

FINISHING

21. Fill any screw holes or imperfections in the wood with wood filler.

22. Thoroughly sand all of the wood parts on the completed bathroom cabinet.

23. Stain or paint the bathroom cabinet the color of your choice. We painted our cabinet a bright white.

24. Install the drawer pull on the bathroom cabinet door.

25. Use two cabinet hinges to attach the door to the bathroom cabinet. It will be necessary to chisel out a thin rectangle of wood, the length of the hinge and slightly less deep than the closed hinge is thick, on the edge of the cabinet door to accommodate each of the cabinet hinges. If necessary, install a small magnetic catch to keep the door closed.

26. You may hang your bathroom cabinet by screwing directly through the back into studs in an appropriate wall, as we did. If you cannot find suitable studs, use molly bolts to anchor the cabinet securely.

14. Each of the top/bottoms (G) will be centered sideways on the open ends of the cabinet assembly and placed flush with the back of the cabinet, as shown in figure 6. Apply glue to the ends of the side assembly and the edge of the back, and nail through the cabinet top/bottoms into the edges of the back and side assemblies, using 1½-inch (4d) finish nails spaced every 4 inches.

MAKING THE DOOR

15. The cabinet door, like the sides of the cabinet, is a 1 x 2 frame that has been dadoed in the center to accommodate a piece of glass.

16. Cut two door sides (G) from the remaining dadoed 1 x 2 pine, each measuring 21⅞ inches long.

17. Miter each end of both door sides (G) at opposing 45-degree angles, as shown in figure 2. Make certain that the dadoed edge is on the short side of each piece.

18. Cut two door top/bottoms (H) from the dadoed 1 x 2 pine, each measuring 17⅞ inches long.

OCCASIONAL FURNITURE

Fern Pedestal

We searched high and low for a substantial-looking pedestal for our favorite fern. The ones we found were either too skimpy looking or so expensive that it would require a second mortgage on our home to purchase one. This pedestal is not only good looking, but really cheap to build.

fern pedestal

Materials

- 1 sheet (4' x 8') of ⅜" plywood
- 12 linear feet of 1 x 2 pine
- 15 linear feet of 5¼" crown molding
- 12 linear feet of ¾" screen molding

Hardware

- 24 1½" screws
- 60 1¼" screws
- Handful of 1" (2d) finish nails

Cutting List

Code	Description	Qty.	Materials	Dimensions
A	Long Support	6	1 x 2 pine	11¼" long
B	Short Support	6	1 x 2 pine	9¾" long
C	Narrow Side	2	⅜" plywood	11¼" x 48"
D	Wide Side	2	⅜" plywood	12" x 48"
E	Top/Bottom	2	⅜" plywood	20" x 20"

MAKING THE INNER SUPPORTS

1. Because it is made of relatively thin plywood, the pedestal requires inner supports. Cut six long supports (A) from 1 x 2 pine, each measuring 11¼ inches long.

2. Cut six short supports (B) from 1 x 2 pine, each measuring 9¾ inches long.

3. Place two long supports (A) on a level surface, parallel to each other and 9¾ inches apart. Fit two short supports (B) between the ends of the two long supports (A), as shown in figure 1. Screw through the long supports (A) into the ends of the short supports (B), using two 1½-inch screws on each joint.

4. Repeat step 3 twice to construct two more support assemblies.

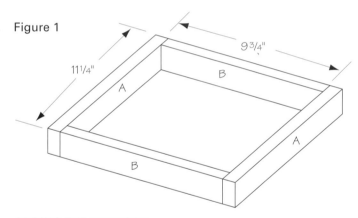

Figure 1

ADDING THE PLYWOOD

5. Cut two narrow sides (C) of ⅜-inch plywood, each measuring 11¼ x 48 inches. Make certain that you cut the plywood so that the surface design runs along the 48-inch length.

6. Place the three support assemblies, short inner support (B) side down, on a level surface, parallel to each other and 21¾ inches apart. Fit one narrow side (C) over the three support assemblies, as shown in figure 2. The two outer support assemblies should be flush with the ends of the narrow side (C). Apply glue to the meeting surfaces, and screw through the narrow side (C) into the support assemblies, using three 1¼-inch screws on each joint.

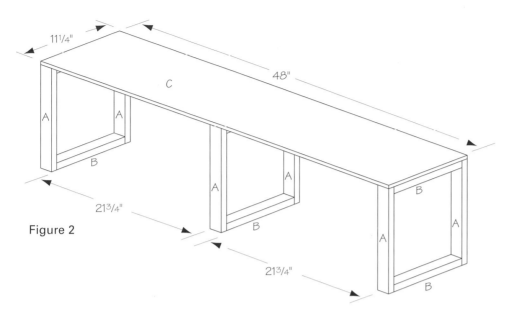

Figure 2

7. Repeat step 2 to attach the remaining narrow side (C) to the opposite side of the three support assemblies.

8. Cut two wide sides (D) from ⅜-inch plywood, each measuring 12 x 48 inches. Again, make certain that the plywood design runs with the 48-inch length.

9. Place the support assemblies and attached narrow sides (C) on a level surface. Fit one wide side (D) over the edges of the narrow sides (C). Apply glue to the support assemblies and the edges of the narrow sides. Screw through the wide side (D) into the support assemblies, using three 1¼-inch screws on each joint, and nail through the wide side (D) into the edges of the narrow sides (C), using 1-inch (2d) finishing nails spaced every 6 inches.

10. Repeat step 5 to attach the remaining wide side (D) to the support assemblies.

ADDING THE TOP AND BOTTOM

11. Cut two top/bottoms (E) from ⅜-inch exterior plywood, each measuring 20 x 20 inches.

12. Center one top/bottom over one open end of the pedestal assembly, so that the top/bottom extends 4 inches over each of the plywood sides. Apply glue to the meeting surfaces, and screw through the top/bottom (E) into the support assembly using three 1¼-inch screws on each side.

13. Repeat step 2 to attach the remaining top/bottom (E) to the other open end of the pedestal assembly.

ADDING THE MOLDING

14. Carefully cut and fit the crown molding on all four sides of the top and bottom of the completed planter. It should be attached to the top/bottom (E) and the sides of the pedestal. Apply glue to the meeting surfaces, and use 1-inch (2d) finish nails about every 3 inches. Make sure the nails don't go through the top/bottoms (E).

15. Cut and fit ¾-inch screen molding to cover the exposed plywood edges of the top/bottom (E). Apply glue to the molding, and use 1-inch (2d) finish nails about every 3 inches.

FINISHING

16. Fill any cracks, crevices, or screw holes with wood filler and thoroughly sand all surfaces of the completed pedestal.

17. Seal and paint or stain your pedestal the color of your choice.

Display Shelves

If you have been looking for a great way to display your collection, here's the answer! These display shelves can be built with scrap wood and some pre made trim. Then paint them the color of your choice, and hang them on a prominent wall.

Materials

- 1 linear foot of 1 x 8 pine
- 4 linear feet of beaded molding, 4" wide and ½" thick

Hardware

- 14 1¼" (3d) finish nails
- 8 ¾" wire brads

Cutting List

Code	Description	Qty	Materials	Dimensions
A	Top	1	1 x 8 pine	11" long
B	Front/Back	2	4"-wide beaded molding, ½" thick	12" long
C	Sides	2	4" wide beaded molding, ½" thick	8¼" long

BUILDING THE SIDES

1. Cut one top (A) from 1 x 8 pine, measuring 11 inches long.

2. Cut two front/backs (B) from 4-inch-wide beaded molding, each measuring 12 inches long.

3. Set each of the two front/backs (B) on edge and miter both ends across their width at opposing 45-degree angles, as shown in figure 1. Make certain that the beaded side of the molding is on the outside of the miter.

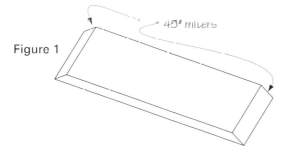

Figure 1

45° miters

4. Cut two sides (C) from 1 x 6 pine, each measuring 8¼ inches long.

5. Set each of the two sides (C) on edge, and miter both ends across their width at opposing 45-degree angles, as shown in figure 1.

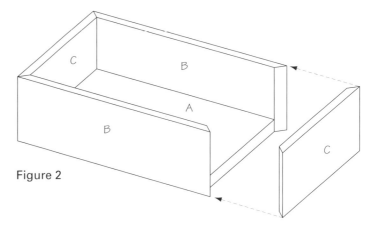

Figure 2

6. Place the top (A) on a level surface. Place the two front/backs (B) on edge on either side of the top (A), matching the 11-inch-long sides, as shown in figure 2. Apply glue to the meeting surfaces and nail through the front/backs (B) into the edges of the top (A), using four evenly spaced 1¼-inch (3d) finish nails on each joint.

7. Place the two sides (C) between the ends of the two front/backs (B), matching miters. Apply glue to the miters, and nail through the sides (C) into the ends of the top (A), using three 1¼-inch (3d) finish nails on each joint. Also nail through each of the mitered corners, using two ¾-inch wire brads on each joint.

FINISHING

8. Fill any screw holes or imperfections in the wood with wood filler.

9. Thoroughly sand the display shelf.

10. Stain or paint the display shelf the color of your choice. We chose an off-white paint to match our walls.

11. To hang the display shelves, simply screw through the underside of the shelf into the wall. Make certain that you either screw into a stud or use appropriate load-bearing hardware such as molly bolts.

Occasional Table

Everyone needs an extra table somewhere in the house, and this table is an extremely versatile one. It is small enough that it can be placed anywhere, but large enough to accommodate a lamp, books, and a plant. You can coordinate the tile and stain colors to match any fabric in your decorating scheme.

Materials

- 45 linear feet of 1 x 4 pine
- 1 piece of ½-inch plywood, 24 inches square
- 4 ceramic tiles*, nominal 12" square
- Tile mastic
- Tile grout
- Grout sealer

* Notes on Materials

The dimensions of the top of this table depend on the size of the ceramic tile you use. If you choose a different size tile, you will have to change the lengths of several pieces. Lay out your tiles in a square pattern and measure the size of the center top (G), allowing grout space between and outside the tiles. Besides the center top (G), you will have to adjust the lengths of pieces A, B, E, and F.

Hardware

- 16   1" (2d) finish nails
- 40   1¼" screws
- 48   1½" screws
- 12   2" screws

Special Tools and Techniques

- 3 or 4 large bar clamps or pipe clamps
- Trowel
- Rubber-surfaced trowel
- Tile cutter (if necessary)*
- Miters

Cutting List

Code	Description	Qty	Materials	Dimensions
A	Long Base	2	1 x 4 pine	24" long
B	Short Base	2	1 x 4 pine	22½" long
C	Wide Leg	4	1 x 4 pine	24" long
D	Narrow Leg	4	1 x 4 pine, ripped	24" long
E	Lower Trim	4	1 x 4 pine	27½" long
F	Upper Trim	4	1 x 4 pine	31" long
G	Center Top	1	½-inch plywood	24" square

BUILDING THE BASE

1. Cut two long bases (A) from 1 x 4 pine, each measuring 24 inches long.

2. Cut two short bases (B) from 1 x 4 pine, each measuring 22½ inches long.

3. Place the two short bases (B) on a level surface, parallel to each other and 22½ inches apart. Fit the two long bases (A) over the ends of the two short bases (B), as shown in figure 1. Screw through the long bases (A) into the ends of the short bases (B), using two 1½-inch screws on each joint.

4. Cut four wide legs (C) from 1 x 4 pine, each measuring 24 inches long.

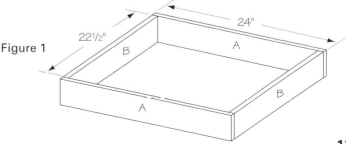

Figure 1

5. Rip a total of 9 feet of 1 x 4 pine to a width of 2¾ inches.

6. Cut four narrow legs (D) from the 2¾-inch-wide material, each measuring 24 inches long.

7. Attach one narrow leg (D) to one wide leg (C) as shown in figure 2. Screw through the wide leg (C) into the edge of the narrow leg (D) using five evenly spaced 1½-inch screws. If you have large enough clamps, apply glue to the edge of the narrow leg (D), clamp the wide leg (C) in place, and let dry for an hour. In this case you may omit the screws. The finished leg assembly should measure 3½ inches across each of the outside widths.

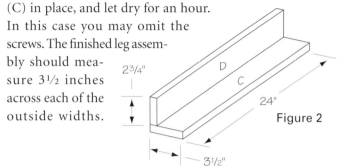

Figure 2

8. Repeat step 7 three more times using the remaining three narrow legs (D) and three wide legs (C).

9. Place the base assembly (A and B) on a level surface. Attach the four leg assemblies to each of the four corners of the base assembly, as shown in figure 3. Apply glue to the meeting surfaces, and screw through both sides of each leg assembly, using two 1¼-inch screws on each side of each leg. Use a try square to make sure that each leg is square to the adjoining base piece.

Figure 3

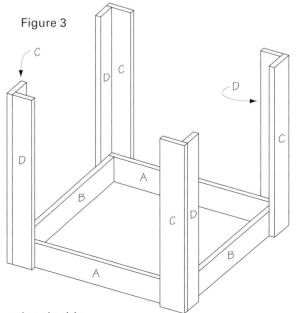

MAKING THE TOP

10. Cut four lower trims (E) from 1 x 4 pine, each measuring 27½ inches long.

11. Miter the ends of each of the four lower trims (E) at opposing 45-degree angles, as shown in figure 4.

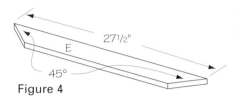

Figure 4

12. Attach each of the lower trims (E) to the base assembly, as shown in figure 5. Apply glue to the top edge of the long and short bases (A and B), and screw through the lower trims (E) into the wide and narrow legs (C and D) and the long and short bases (A and B). Use 1½-inch screws spaced about 6 inches apart. The lower trims should overhang the legs by 1 inch. Use 1¼-inch (3d) finish nails to keep the outside corners of the miter joints aligned. Nail across the joint from each side, starting about ¾ inch from the end. Offset the nails slightly to avoid hitting the first nail with the second one.

Figure 5

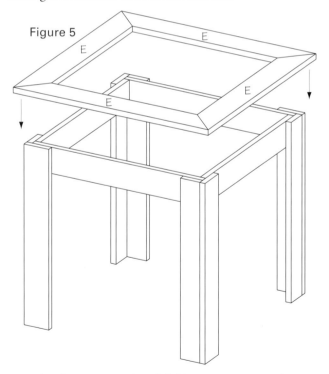

13. Cut four upper trims (F) from 1 x 4 pine, each measuring 31 inches long.

14. Miter the ends of each of the four upper trims (F) at opposing 45-degree angles, as shown in figure 4.

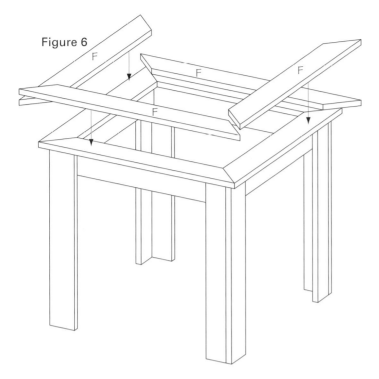

Figure 6

F F F F

15. Lay the four upper trims (F) on top of the lower trims (E) to check the miter joints, as shown in figure 6. The upper trims (F) should extend outside the lower trims (E) by 1¾ inches, and the miters of the upper trims (F) should line up with the miters of the lower trims (E). Mark the placement of the inside edges of the upper trims (F), remove the upper trims (F), and apply glue to the portion of the lower trims (E) outside the marks. Clamp the upper trims (F) in place, and let the glue cure for about an hour. If you are short of clamps, screw through each lower trim (E) into its upper trim (F), using three 1¼ inch screws. You can then move your clamps to the next pair of trims and fasten them together. Again, use 1¼-inch (3d) finish nails to keep the outside corners of the miter joints aligned. Nail across the joint from each side, starting about ¾ inch from the end. Offset the nails slightly to avoid hitting the first nail with the second one.

16. Cut one center top (G) from ½ inch-thick plywood, measuring 24 inches square.

17. Fit the center top (G) in the center of the four upper trims (F). Screw through the center top (G) and the lower trims (E) into the edges of the long and short bases (A and B). Use 2-inch screws, three to a side, placed ⅜ inch from the edges of the center top (G).

ADDING THE TILE

18. Following the manufacturer's directions carefully, spread an even coat of tile mastic over the surface of the plywood top (G) with a trowel.

19. Place the four tiles on the mastic one at a time, making sure that they are absolutely straight, and that the spaces between the tiles are all the same. Do not slide them, or the mastic will be forced up on the sides of the tile. Let the mastic dry overnight.

20. Mix the tile grout according the manufacturer's directions (or use premixed grout).

21. Spread the grout over the tile using a rubber-surfaced trowel. Work in an arc, and hold the trowel at an angle so that the grout is forced evenly into the spaces between the tiles.

22. When the grout begins to set up, use a damp rag to wipe the excess from the tiles and the joints. If you let it dry, the hardened grout will be very difficult to remove. The idea is to use as little water as possible when removing the excess so that you don't thin the grout that remains. Let the grout dry overnight.

23. Rinse the remaining film from the tile and wipe it with an old towel.

24. Apply grout sealer, following the manufacturer's directions. Many grout sealers recommend that you wait several days before applying it to the project.

FINISHING

25. Fill any screw holes or imperfections in the wood with wood filler.

26. Thoroughly sand all of the wood parts on the completed occasional table.

27. Stain or paint the wood portions of the table the color of your choice. We chose a deep burgundy stain to coordinate with our chair.

Bookcase

Everyone can use just one more bookcase. This one is just the right height to place next to a bed, in a bathroom, or (as we did) on a lonely wall in the dining room. It is only a foot deep, so it will hold lots of items without interfering in high-traffic areas.

Materials List

- 12 linear feet of 1 x 12 pine
- 4 wooden circles, approximately 3½" in diameter

Hardware

- 32 1½" screws

Cutting List

Code	Description	Qty.	Materials	Dimensions
A	Top/Bottom	2	1 x 12 pine	30" long
B	Sides	2	1 x 12 pine	24" long
C	Shelf	1	1 x 12 pine	28½" long
D	Feet	4	wooden circles	3½" in diameter

ASSEMBLING THE BOOKCASE

1. Cut two top/bottoms (A) from 1 x 12 pine, each measuring 30 inches long.

2. Cut two sides (B) from 1 x 2 pine, each measuring 24 inches long.

3. Place the two top/bottoms (A) parallel to each other and 24 inches apart. Fit the two sides (B) between the top/bottoms (A), as shown in figure 1. Screw through the top/bottoms (A) into the ends of the sides (B). Use four 1½-inch screws on each of the four joints.

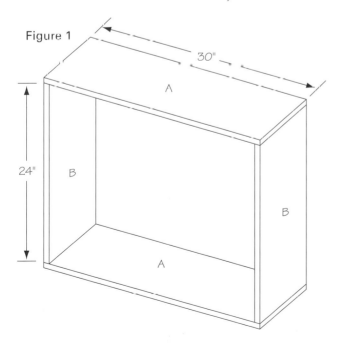

Figure 1

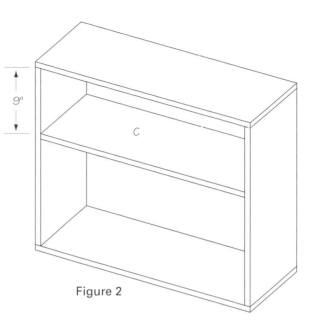

Figure 2

4. Cut one shelf (C) from 1 x 12 pine, measuring 28½ inches long.

5. Fit the shelf (C) into the assembly, as shown in figure 2. Pick the best-looking top/bottom surface and designate it as the "top" of the assembly. We placed our shelf 9 inches from the "top," but that measurement can be altered as you wish. Screw through the sides (B) into the ends of the shelf (C). Use four 1½-inch screws on each of the two joints.

6. Screw the four feet (D) onto the bottom, even with the outside edges of the completed bookcase using 1½-inch-long screws.

FINISHING

7. Fill the screw holes, crevices, and cracks with wood filler.

8. Sand all surfaces of the completed bookcase.

9. Stain or paint the bookcase the color of your choice. We chose to retain the natural color of the pine and simply seal it with a gloss polyurethane.

ACKNOWLEDGMENTS

**If this book is a success,
much of the credit will belong
to people other than the authors.
Our thanks to:**

Thomas Stender

(STENDER DESIGN, CHICAGO, IL)

*Editor Extraordinaire, who patiently waded through
the manuscript and made it right, and whose
illustrations made it comprehensible.*

Chris Bryant

(ALTAMONT PRESS, ASHEVILLE, NC)

*for his inspired art direction, production,
and photographic direction.
What a joy to work with a pro!*

Evan Bracken

(LIGHT REFLECTIONS, HENDERSONVILLE, NC)

*for his photographic genius and never-failing
good humor and patience.*

Patti Kertz

(LONGBOAT KEY, FL)

*for her gracious assistance with photography.
You're becoming a regular in the
acknowledgment section.*

Dan Collett

(BRADENTON, FL)

*for his assistance with photography.
He moved and toted and kept us all in good humor.*

Charlene Foy

(LONGBOAT KEY, FL)

*for her assistance with photography.
You made us look good when we didn't!*

Metric Conversion Chart

To convert inches to centimeters,
multiply the number of inches by 2.5

To convert feet to meters,
divide the number of feet by 3.25

INCHES	CM	INCHES	CM
1/8	.5	12	31
1/4	1	13	33.5
3/8	1.25	14	36
1/2	1.5	15	38.5
5/8	1.75	16	41
3/4	2	17	44
7/8	2.25	18	46
1	2.5	19	49
1 1/4	3.5	20	51
1 1/2	4	21	54
1 3/4	4.5	22	56.5
2	5	23	59
2 1/2	6.5	24	62
3	8	25	64
3 1/2	9	26	67
4	10	27	69
4 1/2	11.5	28	72
5	13	29	74.5
5 1/2	14	30	77
6	15	31	79.5
7	18	32	82
8	21	33	85
9	23	34	87
10	26	35	90
11	28	36	92.5

Index

LARK BOOKS

FOR A FREE CATALOG
of our complete line of distinctive craft books,
write to
Lark Books
50 College Street
Asheville, NC 28801
Or in the continental U.S. and Canada
call 1-800-284-3388

WEBSITE: www.larkbooks.com
E-MAIL: larkmail@larkbooks.com

RELATED TITLES

2x4 Furniture

by Stevie Henderson

(Sterling/Lark, 1993)
136 pages, 29 color photographs,
100 b&w illustrations, paperback,
$14.95 (CAN $20.95)

ISBN 0-8069-0294-9

Great-Looking 2x4 Furniture

by Stevie Henderson with Mark Baldwin

(Sterling/Lark, 1996)
128 pages, 50 color photographs,
120 b&w illustrations, hardback,
$27.95 (CAN $38.95)

ISBN 0-8069-8162-8

Great Outdoor 2x4 Furniture

by Stevie Henderson with Mark Baldwin

(Lark Books, 1998)
128 pages, 44 color photographs,
120 b&w illustrations, paperback,
$21.95, (CAN $29.95)

ISBN 1-57990-047-X